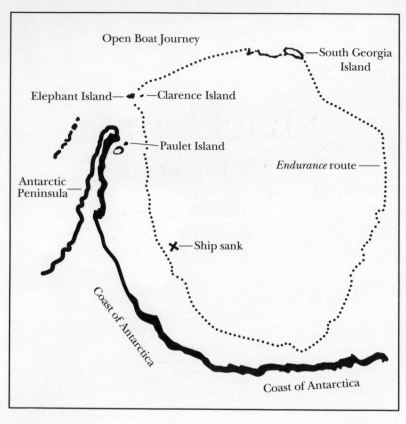

Open Boat Journey

South Georgia Island

Elephant Island — • —Clarence Island

—Paulet Island

Endurance route —

Antarctic
Peninsula—

✗—Ship sank

Coast of Antarctica

Coast of Antarctica

Weddell Sea Area

Shackleton
of the Antarctic

T. H. BAUGHMAN

UNIVERSITY OF NEBRASKA PRESS
LINCOLN AND LONDON

Library of Congress Cataloging-in-Publication Data

Baughman, T. H., 1947–
Shackleton of the Antarctic / T. H. Baughman.
p. cm.
Originally published: Tallahassee, Fla.:
Eöthen Press, c2002.
Includes bibliographical references.
ISBN 978-0-8032-1944-1 (pbk.: alk. paper)
1. Shackleton, Ernest Henry, Sir,
1874–1922—Travel—Antarctica.
2. Endurance (Ship) 3. Imperial Trans-Antarctic
Expedition (1914–1917) 4. Antarctica—Discovery
and exploration—British. I. Title.
G850 1914.S53 B38 2009
919.8'904—dc22
2009007966

TO:

*I have been fortunate to know
many wonderful people in my life,
but I have never met a better man
than Kenny L. Brown*

AND TO:

*Peter Harrison, whose example
inspires me every day to be
and do my best*

CONTENTS

PREFACE

Woodrow Wilson once apologized to his audience for giving a two-hour lecture—he said that he had not had time to prepare a twenty-minute one. Clearly, attempting to write a biography of one hundred pages to tell the life that others have struggled to fit into seven hundred pages is a different type of effort.

For some time, friends and colleagues have asked me to write this type of account. My lectures on Shackleton around the world have been very kindly received, and the hope was that I could transfer some of that enthusiasm on to the printed page. Having tried, I can only hope that some readers will think I have succeeded.

Unlike my three other books on Antarctic history, this volume clearly is not a contribution of original research. It is, instead, an attempt to provide the reader with a short account of the entire life of this explorer rather than merely focusing on the *Endurance* expedition, as some who have come to that story for a quick buck and then moved on to other pursuits have provided. Unless the reader appreciates the explorer's early life, the actual achievements of both the *Endur-*

ance and *Nimrod* expeditions are diminished. Shackleton's greatness was forged upon the events of the *Discovery* expedition.

My purpose here is straightforward: to provide the reader with an introduction to the person who is now the most famous of the Antarctic explorers and to provide a first book for someone seeking to delve into Antarctic history as a whole.

The publication of a book affords the opportunity to acknowledge some of the people who have helped so much in all my scholarly efforts. At my present institution I draw inspiration from the example set by several of my colleagues whose scholarly production I admire but could never hope to match: Xiao-bing Li, Wei Chen, and Kevin Hayes. In the larger sphere of polar work, no one has been more inspirational than Peter Harrison or more useful than John Splettstoesser. That I am unable to share more time with either man is a tragedy for me. I thank J. David Macey, Karen Soeltz, James Wells, Michael and Julie McBride, and Michael Rosove, the preeminent American historian, for reading drafts of this book. Among my colleagues at my university I would like to thank Diane and Kenny L. Brown and Chris and William Radke for their many contributions to my life and my work.

I would not be able to write about my subject without the firsthand experience I have gained in the field. For making such opportunities available to me and for providing insights into other disciplines that enrich my work I thank Charlie and Victoria Wheatley, Pat Abbott, Peter Carey, and, finally, Robert and Charlene Wilkinson, as Bob was the one who provided my original entrée into the polar regions. Henry Pollack and I have sailed together enough that we are practically a vaudeville team, and he taught me much about earth sciences and how to be an academic administrator. As always, I acknowledge the contributions of Judith and Richard L. Greaves to my work.

I want to single out the quality of leadership exemplified by Mike Messick, Matt Drennan, and Charles "Trip" Dennis, three men with whom Shackleton would have been proud to have sailed.

Finally, I cannot fail to remember Dr. Ian M. Whillans, world-renowned glaciologist, who gave me my first chance to go to Antarctica as a token humanist. For those of us fortunate enough to have served under him on scientific expeditions, he was our Shackleton. Ian was my hero.

INTRODUCTION

Twenty-eight men stood on a desolate Antarctic ice floe one thousand miles from the nearest human contact. In a few months the ice would melt. To survive they would have to be safely on land before that happened--if they did not starve first. The odds were stacked against them. They faced all the horrors that the Antarctic could bring to bear: numbing cold and the worst weather on the globe. They could freeze, starve, or drown. They had a single advantage, however—one that proved decisive. They were led by Shackleton.

This saga is their tale and the story of the man who led them.

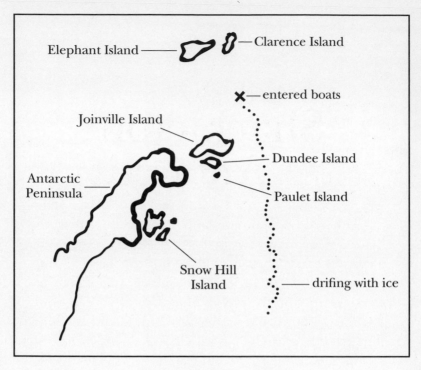

Elephant Island —— Clarence Island

✖—— entered boats

Joinville Island

Antarctic
Peninsula ——

—— Dundee Island

Paulet Island

Snow Hill
Island

—— drifing with ice

The Antarctic Peninsula

Shackleton
of the Antarctic

ONE

Discovery

Although set in the Antarctic, the greatest adventure of all time began off the coast of Africa, on a steamer carrying British soldiers out to the Anglo-Boer War. This conflict pitted the most powerful empire on earth, Great Britain, against a small nation of a few million Boers and showed that in the twentieth century determined smaller nations might hold their own even against the most powerful nation states.

A chance occurrence signaled the start of this story. An affable and gregarious Anglo-Irish third officer befriended a young soldier, Cedric Longstaff, who was returning to the battlefields. They began a friendship during the long relaxed days at sea that allowed opportunities for pleasant discussions of favorite topics. Hundreds of similar acquaintances grew up on dozens of other ships plying the sea lane between England and South Africa, but unlike those other friendships, this one changed the course of Antarctic history.

The young third officer's name was Ernest Shackleton (1874–1922), and although exploring the south polar regions may not yet have entered his mind, other ideas had. He wanted to be famous and he wanted to be wealthy enough to enjoy life. The venue for success was immaterial—politics, literature, or business were all the same to him. Recently he had acquired an additional motivation to seek fame and fortune—he had met the woman he would marry, and he wanted a financially assured future for them both.

Returning from one of his cruises, Shackleton saw a newspaper article describing the National Antarctic Expedition and thought it a possibility for fame and adventure. The newspaper noted that the principal patron of the endeavor was Llewellyn Longstaff, a name Shackleton recognized as that of the father of the man he had befriended en route to South Africa.

Correspondence between the elder Longstaff and Shackleton resulted in Longstaff putting Shackleton's name forth as one of the officers of the ship; the primogenitor of the expedition, Sir Clements R. Markham (1830–1916), had little choice but to agree to naming Shackleton to the expedition. The adventure had begun.

Given the importance of the *Discovery* expedition to Shackleton's personality and career, a brief account of it is appropriate here. From the time that Sir Clements became the president of the Royal Geographical Society (RGS) in 1893, he was determined to launch a great national Antarctic expedition, officered and manned by the Royal Navy. Markham had been part of the voyages of the Royal Navy in the Arctic in the nineteenth century and sought to repeat what he perceived as great successes in the north polar regions with new adventures in the South.

Markham was a determined and stubborn old man. Although few would argue today that the British navy's activities in the Arctic in the nineteenth century were successful, Markham believed that polar work was a superb training ground for naval officers, and this proposal matched his ideas about romantic exploration. To use naval personnel was central to his plan, but by the time the crew of the *Discovery* had been assembled, several key players were not from the Royal Navy.

Two individuals stand out most clearly: Albert B. Armitage (1864–1943) and Shackleton. The choice of both was influenced by wealthy patrons—the second largest donor, newspaper magnate Alfred Harmsworth, recommended Armitage—and Markham again acquiesced to the wishes of those who had funded the endeavor. Armitage was appointed pilot, a title that moved him out of control of the ship's day-to-day affairs in favor of a Royal Navy lieutenant, Charles Royds (1876–1930), while Shackleton, the other non-naval man, was appointed third officer.

The *Discovery* expedition played an important part in making Shackleton a famed explorer. Markham chose Robert Falcon Scott (1868–1912) to lead the *Discovery* expedition, which was to be a largely naval effort with government support, to the south polar regions.

Scott was to cooperate with contemporaneous Swedish, German, and Scottish national expeditions. In July 1901 Shackleton departed on the *Discovery*, which had been built specifically for this endeavor. The expedition was to be away only two summers and a winter since lack of funding prohibited a longer stay.

From the beginning of the voyage Shackleton proved an immensely popular member of the expedition. Scott put Shackleton's experience in sailing ships as well as his skills in handling cargo to good use. Always willing to take on whatever task was at hand, Shackleton impressed his captain with his talents and his affability.

The *Discovery* sailed to McMurdo Sound and established a base at Hut Point on Ross Island. A range of scientific work was begun that fall and continued through the winter.

The major event of the *Discovery* expedition was an attempt on the South Pole. Scott planned to lead this trip himself and chose as his companions Edward A. Wilson (1872–1912), who became one of the legendary figures of the Heroic Era of Antarctic exploration (1901–22), and his young third officer, Shackleton.

The trio set out 2 November 1902, accompanied

for the first week by a support party. When that group turned back the three men were on their own, assisted in their southward trek only by eighteen dogs.

Much has been written about Scott's lack of skill in dog sledging. Little else needs to be said other than that he put Shackleton, who had never worked with dogs, in charge of the animals. Still, the dogs pulled the sledges southward, assisted by the men who were manhauling, whereby humans tied ropes around their bodies, over the shoulder and waist usually, and attached a line to a sledge. By this means they pulled the supplies and equipment over the ice.

Nineteenth-century British Arctic expeditions had used manhauling, and Markham believed it to be the "true British way." That humans, without the modern freeze-dried foodstuffs of today, could not haul sufficient provisions for an assault on the pole—a journey of more than 1,400 miles from winter quarters to the pole and back—was unknown to Markham. When the dogs died, in all likelihood of exhaustion and poisoning from their dried fish diet, the three men struggled on, ironically glad to be rid of the dogs. Since they drove the dogs ineptly, the animals did not perform well.

Scott was determined to get as far as he could before 31 December 1902, the date he fixed in his mind for the last southern camp. Surfaces were so bad that for a month Scott, Shackleton, and Wilson had to relay, pulling one of the two sledges until lunch and then returning to fetch the other to bring it up to the camping place for the night.

The work was exhausting and the food insufficient. Their basic meal was a thick concoction of pemmican, a fatty meat soup. Inadequately nourished by their food, the men first used up their body fat. Continuing on, their bodies began to consume themselves for fuel. They were cold, suffering from exposure, and as the days wore on their minds fixated on food. In addition, they were dehydrated because scarce fuel supplies limited the amount of water they could melt for drinking.

By mid-December their appearance was gaunt. Each step was a struggle, yet they pushed on for "King and Country," only to have another disaster overtake them: scurvy. Even though in the eighteenth century Captain James Cook (1728–79) had sailed around the world and made voyages to Antarctica without a scurvy problem, the disease was still poorly understood in the late nineteenth century. At the time Scott sailed, many scientists believed that scurvy was caused by a toxin in badly canned meat; regrettably Scott, Wilson, and Shackleton labored under this erroneous information.

By late December 1902 all three men showed signs of scurvy, but Shackleton was clearly the most seriously afflicted. Wilson, a physician, noted the problem and reported it to Scott. After changing their diet from what the captain perceived to be tainted food, all three seemed to improve.

Scott was overly optimistic, and when the trio turned north from 82°16′ S, Shackleton's health problems worsened: he was coughing blood and suffering from shortness of breath. Shackleton's health continued to deteriorate. Scott prudently stopped his lieutenant from pulling the sledge. The northbound party rigged a sail in a following wind to help propel their sledge; at one point Shackleton rode on the vehicle both to help steer it and to rest.

Shackleton's health waxed and waned on the way back to the ship. By the time they returned to the *Discovery*, all three men were in very bad shape, but Shackleton was the worst. Scott was up and about fairly quickly, while Shackleton recovered more slowly, and Wilson was plagued for a month with a leg ailment related to the scurvy.

Even though Shackleton appeared to be recovering, Scott invalided him home on the relief ship in January 1903. This change in fortune—to be sent home on Scott's opinion that Shackleton's constitution was not up to the rigors of polar work—was the defining moment in Shackleton's life. He returned to England in 1903 determined to prove not only that he was *fit* to survive but that he could *succeed* in the Antarctic. Shackleton had found his goal in life—to lead an Antarctic expedition. His route to fame and fortune was now settled: he lacked only the financial wherewithal to make his dream a reality.

TWO

On the Move

Upon his return from the *Discovery* expedition, Shackleton abandoned his career in the merchant marines and sought employment on land. For a few months he foundered until he received help from someone who was to become one of his staunchest supporters throughout his career: H. R. Mill (1861–1951), the former librarian of the Royal Geographical Society and the premier polar historian of the early twentieth century.

Shackleton was not alone in turning to Mill for help. William S. Bruce (1867–1921), the gifted Scottish scientist-explorer, had benefited from Mill's help at various times in his career. Scott, too, counted Mill as a benefactor and acknowledged his gratitude to the older man.[1] Mill knew all the polar explorers of the first half of the twentieth century, and their correspondence proves that Mill was a friend, mentor, and, at times, protector. Indeed Mill deserves the title "Friend to Heroes."[2]

Shackleton was the next to be numbered among Mill's friends. Mill helped him secure a position as secretary (executive director) of the Royal Scottish Geographical Society. This conservative organization was a strange place for the breezy and gregarious Shackleton. When he wanted to install a telephone in the office, eyebrows were raised. When he was caught practicing his golf swing in the office, the leaders of the society were not amused. When he wanted to be more aggressive in marketing the institution, the Fellows of the RSGS thought the idea a bit too forward. Shackleton and the Society soon parted company.

As a returning Antarctic hero Shackleton was a much sought-after personality. His polar mantle brought him into contact with many prominent figures in business, society, and politics in the months following his return to Britain. Shackleton was not shy about declaring his desire to return to Antarctica at the head of his own expedition. To do that he needed a convenient millionaire eager to gain glory by patronizing such an endeavor. Try as he might, however, he could not find one.

He tried other schemes instead. Tobacco sales seemed to promise a bright future, but the business adventure did not pan out. A dreamer like Shackleton could find few things more appealing than gold and all that it symbolized in terms of quick wealth. Eastern European gold had a particularly appealing ring to an adventurer like Shackleton, but again his projects came to nothing.

The Russo-Japanese war had recently come to an end, and the Russians had thousands of soldiers in the Far East whom the government wanted repatriated to Europe. Shackleton took part in a hastily organized venture that offered to return the troops on a per-person basis: £40 for officers, £12 for enlisted men. The offer came to nothing.

Someone even suggested that Shackleton run for parliament, and enough people agreed with the idea that Shackleton's name was put forth as a Unionist candidate in a district in which the party was not favored. Shackleton was brilliant on the campaign trail, and audiences loved him, but in the end he came out third in the poll. Shackleton's own dry assessment was that he had gotten all the applause but someone else had gotten all the votes.

Nothing he did was bringing him closer to his dream. He was getting old for an explorer; at the close of 1905 he was already thirty-one. He had a wife and a child; another child followed in December 1906. Perhaps the dreamer needed to face reality.

At that dispirited point in his life, one of the men he met and impressed was William Beardmore, a Scottish industrialist who manufactured iron plating for battleships. In the early twentieth century this growth industry was spurred on by advances in naval architecture—the first dreadnought battleship, faster and more powerful than anything else afloat, had been launched 10 February 1906. Germany was a nation on the rise and sought to build a great fleet to rival and, so the British thought, to threaten British supremacy on the seas. Beardmore became a rich man by producing the products needed for the Anglo-German naval rivalry.

The Scottish manufacturer approached Shackleton about a job. Shackleton was offered a position as secretary to a commission that the company was undertaking to study gas engine design.[3] At the same time, Beardmore was aware of the reflected glory that would shine upon his company should a hero with Shackleton's personality represent the business in certain social situations. With the job offer, however, came a question: Had he put the foolishness of another Antarctic expedition out of his head? Shackleton said that he had and went to work for Beardmore in late 1905.

No doubt the former explorer meant to keep his word. He performed his assigned duties well and proficiently, and in later years Beardmore remembered his employee's work as excellent. Yet how easy it would be to imagine the charismatic Anglo-Irishman at a dinner party chatting away about one thing or another until the conversation turned to the Antarctic. Immediately, one can imagine him becoming alive and animated, enthralling his audience with tales of the great South.

While in Beardmore's employ Shackleton became friends—quite good friends—with Mrs. Beardmore. Historians care little about the sexual life of their subject unless it affects policy or actions. The possibility that Mrs. Beardmore and the charming young explorer's relationship was more than platonic is, however, a reasonable subject for conjecture. While the evidence remains inconclusive, descendants within Beardmore's own family consider it probable that the two were lovers. This possibility might have influenced Beardmore's decision to fund the expedition.

In January 1907 Beardmore told Shackleton that he was willing to guarantee a loan that would allow the explorer to launch his own expedition, one which came to be known as the *Nimrod* expedition, 1907–9. Perhaps Beardmore believed in Shackleton; perhaps he just wanted him out of the way.

Shackleton had his money. His dream was about to become a reality.

THREE

Nimrod

Few men have even one great adventure in their lives; Shackleton had two, each of which surpasses nearly all the dramas of other people. The first of these marvelous occurrences was the *Nimrod* expedition.

Just when Shackleton had nearly given up hope, his luck turned. He was fond of quoting "Prospice," the work of his favorite poet, Robert Browning: "For the worst turns to better for the best." The receipt of Beardmore's promise of money proved Browning right. Preparing for an expedition of this magnitude usually takes years; Shackleton planned to leave in seven months. Those who knew of the difficulties of such arrangements privately scoffed, but Shackleton did it.

During the preparations, one of the greatest moments in polar history took place 11 February 1907, not in any polar region but at Number 1, Savile Row, London, then the home of the Royal Geographical Society. Having gotten word of the assurance of money on a Friday, Shackleton was outside the office of J. Scott Keltie, longtime secretary of the RGS, the following Monday. Shackleton was kept waiting, as Keltie had visitors. Finally the door opened and the young aspirant was admitted. Once inside he found that Keltie's two callers were Fridtjof Nansen (1861–1930) and Roald Amundsen (1872–1928). For a few brief minutes the three greatest explorers of the early twentieth century were together in a single room.

When the other two departed, Shackleton told Keltie of his good fortune. Keltie was surprisingly cool. Shackleton expected him to be more excited since Keltie had long been friendly and encouraging. The interview ended and Shackleton went off to the newspaper offices to announce his plans, which were carried in the daily editions the following day.

Unbeknownst to Shackleton, Keltie's coolness was inspired by the knowledge of a plan by Robert Falcon Scott, Shackleton's old commander, to mount a second expedition. Scott had sworn Keltie to secrecy, and the RGS secretary had complied with what he assumed were Scott's wishes. When the news of Shackleton's plans reached Scott, the latter was livid and sent a blistering letter to Keltie excoriating him for failing to forestall Shackleton's efforts. A lengthy correspondence passed between Scott and the RGS secretary before Scott finally calmed down, at least in regard to Keltie's actions.

Scott believed that Shackleton should have given him prior warning of such a venture and that his former protégé owed everything to his former commander. Scott also feared that Shackleton could not carry off such an enterprise and, in bungling, would make it harder for Scott to raise support for his own expedition. Indeed, at one point Scott compared Shackleton to Carsten E. Borchgrevink (1864–1934), leader of the successful but disregarded *Southern Cross* expedition (1898–1900). Borchgrevink was Scott's model of the worst possible combination of qualities for a polar leader. To compare Shackleton to Borchgrevink was the ultimate insult.[4]

A series of letters passed between Scott and Shackleton. At first Shackleton was conciliatory and seemed willing to placate his old boss, but as the correspondence went on he showed less enthusiasm for agreeing to Scott's demands. Edward Wilson was brought in to mediate the dispute but was unsuccessful. In his ethereal view of the world, Wilson assumed that Shackleton would withdraw from the field once he knew of Scott's plans. Wilson did not understand Shackleton's burning ambition.

In the end a compromise was reached; Shackleton agreed not to use Scott's old headquarters at Hut Point or even to work west of 170° E. This agreement can be justified only by accepting Scott's proprietal view of McMurdo as his own. At the time Shackleton had little choice but to agree, and he did. He asked only to have time to make the changes in his plans public. His supporters had given him money in part because he already knew the route from Hut Point. Shackleton needed time to persuade them to continue to back him with this alteration in his program.

The dispute settled, at least for the time, Shackleton worked to purchase a ship, assemble a crew, and accomplish the thousand tasks essential for an expedition to leave port. Shackleton prided himself as being a quick but accurate judge of men, and for the most part he was successful.

Unlike Scott, Shackleton had no interest in science and saw it as window dressing for the adventure, and yet he chose fine scientists for the expedition. The two most prominent were T. W. Edgeworth David (1858–1934), the doyen of the Australian scientific community, and a young student of David's, Douglas Mawson (1882–1958), who subsequently went on to a brilliant Antarctic career of his own. In addition to these scientists, Shackleton chose Frank Wild (1874–1939), the able-bodied seaman from the *Discovery* cruise who eventually became one of the polar party in 1908.

In 1902, while traveling with Scott and Wilson, Shackleton had seen firsthand how the dogs had failed the men on the barrier. That they had been badly handled by the trio, who knew almost nothing about dog sledging, did not enter into Shackleton's thoughts in planning his own assault on the pole. During the *Discovery* expedition, Albert B. Armitage, who had served in the Arctic on the Jackson-Harmsworth expedition (1894–97), talked about the possibility of using ponies. During the discussions of that first expedition, Shackleton had toyed with the idea of using a motorized vehicle. His invention was literally and figuratively a rum cart fashioned from the empty barrels that had once held the men's daily ration of grog. Though the experiment was a pathetic failure, Reginald Skelton (1872–1952), Scott's thoroughly competent and inventive chief engineer on the *Discovery*, was prompted to speculate:

> I have an idea that a motor car driven by petroleum could be constructed to do very good work on it [the barrier]. Of course the design would have to be greatly different from ordinary cars especially in the matter of wheels and the body would have to be a van to use as a hut. Precautions would have to be taken in case of a breakdown to take sledges and the car could drag a large supply of oil with depots (laid out at intervals). I believe 500 or 600 miles each way could be covered.[5]

Thus Shackleton planned in 1907 to use three modes of transport. As his principal means, he opted for ponies instead of dogs. His patron, William Beardmore, played a crucial role in his decision to take a much-touted automobile. Beardmore had recently acquired the Arrol-Johnson automobile works, a foundering company on the verge of bankruptcy. Eager to see the Scottish automobile industry survive, he urged Shackleton to take one of his vehicles, slightly modified, to the South with him. Newspaper writers loved the idea and proclaimed that Shackleton would ride to the South Pole at speeds unobtainable on ice even today. Despite the sensational public ballyhoo, Shackleton understood the realities of motor travel circa 1907 and privately admitted that the car was mostly for show and that he would depend on ponies and his third means of transport, manhauling.

Manhauling, a seemingly senseless concept absurdly applied, was in Shackleton's case an even greater folly. The polar party would not take skis; they would walk. When the *Discovery* set sail, virtually none of the men had any experience with skis, a form of travel little used in England at the opening of the twentieth century and practiced largely in Scandinavia. Despite this, many on the expedition, both officers and men, became fairly accomplished skiers and quickly saw the benefit of a form of locomotion well suited to ice and snow conditions. Shackleton was a miserable skier, among the worst on the *Discovery*; he would walk.

The crew set sail in the tiny three-hundred-ton *Nimrod* in August 1907. The departure from England had been given additional luster when King Edward VII and Queen Alexandra visited the ship prior to its sail-

ing. The queen gave Shackleton a Union Jack to place
at the South Pole. The ship departed England for Australia, where Shackleton joined it, and then proceeded
on to Christchurch, New Zealand.

In New Zealand, Shackleton, who was chronically
short of funds, continued his attempts to raise money.
He had counted on support from the loyal Austral-
asian colonies. His association with Professor David helped. The fifty-year-old professor was well con-
nected in the Australian colony, which made a grant
of £5,000 to the expedition.

Another problem surfaced in Christchurch. The
Nimrod was so small and so cramped that Shackleton
feared her steaming range would limit his opportunities for exploration and might even make it difficult
for him to find a suitable wintering spot now that he
had sacrificed the McMurdo option. He therefore arranged to have the *Nimrod* towed the first 1,510 miles
south from New Zealand. Having arranged the deal
with the Union Steamship Company, the Anglo-Irishman charmed the directors of the company into providing the service for free.

On the day of departure from Lyttelton, Christchurch's port, crowds lined the dock to see the explorers off to the gelid wastes of the south polar regions.
What they saw was an appallingly heavily loaded craft.
The Plimsoll line (the mark that indicates a ship's
maximum safe load) had disappeared beneath the water, and barely three and a half feet of freeboard re-

mained. Given the threatening waters that awaited them, Shackleton was taking an enormous risk.

Once in open water the *Koonya*, commanded by Captain F. P. Evans, did a masterful job dragging the little *Nimrod* through the water, but both ships soon found themselves in heavy seas that threatened to swamp the small vessel. The crew jettisoned deck cargo, while the *Koonya* spread oil on the water, but Shackleton's vessel still rose and fell with each giant wave, often disappearing from the sight of the towing vessel in the trough of the waves. After 1,510 miles Captain Evans had performed his duty, having commanded the first steel ship to proceed so far south. He cut the line and the men of the *Nimrod* were on their own.

The ocean around Antarctica freezes every winter, doubling the size of the continent with its frozen sea. Each spring the pack ice breaks up, and vessels pushing south must find their way through the open leads until they have passed through the ice that drifts out from the continent to melt in the warmer waters to the north.

Fortunately, the *Nimrod* moved quickly through the pack ice. Eventually, the vessel reached the physical feature that so captured the imagination of nineteenth- and early twentieth-century Antarctic explorers: the Great Ice Barrier, now known as the Ross Ice Shelf. This glacial accumulation of ice is often more than a hundred feet high where it meets the Ross Sea. Larger than France, the Great Ice Barrier flows out into the ocean, where parts of it regularly calve off and float to the north, forming the great flat-topped tabular icebergs so associated with south polar waters. Shackleton had seen the barrier before on the *Discovery* and knew that King Edward VII Land[6] was at the end of the ice shelf, for he had been the officer on watch in 1902 when the ship reached the end of the barrier. This greatest geographical discovery of Scott's first expedition had been made by Shackleton, who now hoped to find safe and accessible winter quarters in its reaches.

As the men of the *Nimrod* sailed eastward along the barrier, Shackleton hoped to find a suitable place to land. He had in mind an indentation in the barrier he had seen on the *Discovery*, but as his ship moved along the ice wall, the embayment he sought was gone — calved — and the ice had gone out to sea sometime in the intervening six years. To have his base camp on a piece of ice that broke off during the winter or the following spring would mean the almost certain loss of all hands. Now Shackleton faced a problem he had not fully anticipated. True, he had garnered the financial support, assembled a crew, and arranged the thousand-and-one details that carried his dream to reality; this was, after all, his expedition. In one critical matter, however, the *Nimrod* was not his ship: the captain, Rupert England (1878–1942), commanded the vessel.

As Shackleton began to plan his expedition in the late winter and early spring 1907, he tried to persuade

William Colbeck (1871–1930) to be his captain. Colbeck was the most experienced British captain for such work, having served on Borchgrevink's *Southern Cross* expedition and as master on the two *Morning* expeditions to relieve the *Discovery*. The *Morning* was a pathetically underpowered little craft, so much so that it was suggested that the captain had to stop the engine to be able to blow the ship's whistle. Colbeck had demonstrated superb seamanship and consummate skill as an ice master in taking the *Morning* south to Scott's winter quarters and bringing her back again both in the 1902–3 and 1903–4 seasons without mishap. But Colbeck refused the offer, and Shackleton had to turn elsewhere.

Shackleton knew Rupert England from the *Discovery* days when England had been the chief officer of the *Morning*, and a fine first officer he was. The *Nimrod*, however, was England's first command, and the transition to captain exposed his shortcomings. As they sailed along the Great Ice Barrier, England became extremely worried about the safety of his ship, a concern that for him overrode every other consideration, including Shackleton's desire to push the little craft to its limits to find suitable winter quarters. As the ship pushed eastward, the ice became more concentrated and the dangers of pushing farther east more apparent. England suggested turning around and heading for waters he knew—McMurdo Sound.

Later in his life many people came to think of Shackleton as calmly infallible. In February 1907, with the summer rapidly fading and the winter in this instance literally closing in around them, ice was forming that threatened to nip the *Nimrod* and keep it in its grasp. England's insistence on heading for McMurdo Sound prompted an angry and, to some degree, uncontrolled response from Shackleton. At one point Shackleton had persuaded England to push farther east, but on a second occasion a heated exchange occurred on the bridge of the ship. Reports later surfaced of a scuffle and of someone being knocked down. Whatever the outcome, England's authority eventually carried the day, and the *Nimrod* turned westward toward relative safety from the ice—and the one harbor forbidden to the *Nimrod* by Shackleton's agreement with Scott.

As the *Nimrod* steamed westward, Shackleton agonized. In a letter to his wife he laid bare his extreme distress at the decision forced upon him both by Captain England and by the ice conditions that prevented him from finding safe winter quarters to the east. The vessel crossed the 170th E. meridian and into Mc-Murdo Sound.

Cape Royds, named by Scott for the first officer of the *Discovery* expedition, was chosen as the winter quarters of the venture, but the expedition leader and his captain soon found other sources of disagreement. Shackleton had to land his men and supplies, and he had to do it quickly. Of the ten ponies he started with, two had died already. Eight remained, and their survival demanded relief from the buffeting they were enduring. Shackleton also needed to be certain that his supplies, including coal for the winter, were off-loaded. Yet while this work was being done in a superbly rapid manner, England angered Shackleton again by his excessive hesitance to keep the *Nimrod* close to shore. Twice England pulled the vessel offshore to safer water in the face of what he assumed to be threatening weather. Shackleton believed England unduly cautious; England felt prudence was paramount.

By 22 February 1908 the materials needed for the winter and following summer were landed, and England prepared to depart. By this time the two principals were clearly at odds with one another, and before the vessel turned north to winter in New Zealand, Shackleton acted. He sent back with the ship a letter in which he ordered England to be fired when the *Nimrod* reached New Zealand. England knew nothing of the content of this letter until he returned to Christchurch and was informed by Shackleton's agent.

Autumn was hard on the shore party, and Shackleton had much to do. At the outset his luck temporarily failed him. En route from New Zealand the ten ponies had taken a terrible beating from the rough seas and confined quarters. Two died en route to the ice. Not known for their intelligence in any clime, four ponies had eaten sand shortly after arrival and died. Shackleton considered six the bare minimum needed for the southern party; now only four remained, and the winter still lay ahead.

By the time the party had arrived at Cape Royds, another significant change in personnel had occurred. Shackleton originally had wanted Professor T. W. E. David to join the expedition for the voyage to the ice and then return to New Zealand with the ship at the end of the summer's cruising season. At what point the decision was made in the minds of the two principals is unclear, but when the ship returned to winter in New Zealand, Professor David remained to overwinter. The power of his personality dominated the scientific staff and was an influence even on Shackleton.

Before the season ended, Shackleton was determined to lay preliminary supply depots on the trail leading south. In addition to the preparations for the big journey in the following spring, members of the winter party added a distinction to their list of accomplishments by making the first ascent of Mt. Erebus, an active volcano and thus a worthy object of study from a scientific standpoint.

During the winter at Cape Royds, the Boss, as Shackleton was known by his men, created the literary magazine *Aurora Australis*, modeled after the *South Polar Times* on the *Discovery* expedition (similar publications existed on British Arctic efforts of the nineteenth century) but with a twist. He brought a printing press; thus, the *Nimrod* team became the first to publish a book on the last continent. *Aurora Australis* was in much the same vein as the *South Polar Times* and contained fiction and accounts of the events of the expedition. Today, original copies fetch a hefty sum, and in many cases expedition members' copies can be identified.

The party passed the winter amiably. In the spring two major sledging parties were mounted. The main project, upon which Shackleton believed the success of the expedition would be judged, was to reach the geographic pole. At the same time, Professor David was directed to lead a three-man team, which included Alistair Mackay and Douglas Mawson, to the south magnetic pole. This latter trip served two purposes. If successful it would copper Shackleton's bets in case the southern party failed to achieve the geographic pole, and the magnetic pole was also a far more important goal from the point of view of science. Getting to the geographical pole, then and now, has little scientific value, but at the turn of the century, knowing the exact location of the magnetic pole would have helped to solve important questions that plagued the world scientific community. The struggle that David, Mackay, and Mawson endured was not without its own glory. After extraordinary tribulations, the trio reached the vicinity of the south magnetic pole 16 January 1909.[7]

As the south polar party prepared for its own effort, no one knew of the fate of David's party. While planting the Union Jack at the magnetic pole would be acclaimed by relatively few, Shackleton had no misconceptions regarding the public imagination: success at the geographical pole was all that mattered. Pole or nothing were his options.

Shackleton waited impatiently for the moment to depart. Although he had hoped to leave earlier, he was forced to delay his departure from Cape Royds until 29 October 1908 and from Hut Point until 3 November 1908 because the ponies could not travel until the weather warmed. The three men Shackleton chose to join him were Frank Wild, J. B. Adams, and Dr. Eric Marshall. From the outset they were engaged in a race against starvation and death to plant the British flag on the last spot on earth. At first the ponies pulled well and hopes were high that the party might succeed, but two items on the opening day of the march foretold the outcome of the race: one hour out, one of the ponies went "dead lame"; that night Shackleton noted in his diary, "we are working to the bare ounce."[8]

Shackleton was cutting it close. The party had a ninety-one-day supply of food and faced 1,500 miles to the pole and back. That meant the group had to average more than sixteen miles a day, not counting time when weather would not permit travel. Even in a good Antarctic summer, some days would be lost to bad weather. Shackleton did not figure such conditions into his plans. Weight requirements limited fuel as well as food, and fuel was required to melt ice or snow for water—a particularly critical requirement given the arid climate of the Antarctic, which is in reality an icy desert.

By 6 November the group decided to cut their already meager food allotment to extend the number of days on the trail beyond ninety-one. The ponies also required additional attention and made demands on fuel supplies. On occasion, the men ate cold suppers to allot the fuel to warming pony food. Unable to disassociate himself from anthropomorphic feelings regarding the ponies, Shackleton bemoaned the inability of the ponies to withstand the drudgery of their work. Marching on short rations from the outset, the men were able to supplement their meager rations after 21 November 1908 when the first of the ponies was shot and its meat added to the men's diet. Eating frozen, raw pony meat for lunch while marching proved only moderately satisfying because it chilled them. As the remaining ponies sank to their bellies as they traversed the worst surfaces, the men struggled on, establishing their return food and fuel depots as they marched forward, struggling against cold and starvation.[9]

Shackleton knew the first part of the route; he had been there in 1902 with Scott and Wilson. The men trudged onward over the endless wastes of the vast domain of ice now called the Ross Ice Shelf. As November came to a close, a new difficulty of monumental proportions loomed ahead of them. Marching ever southward the men saw in the distance a high and seemingly endless mountain range, the Transantarctic mountains.

They began to search for a path through the impasse. The search could have taken weeks. With typical Shackleton luck, one was quickly found—a great glacier that seemed to lead upward in the direction of the pole. The glacier was crevassed and dangerous; prudence required days, or perhaps weeks, of careful probing and scouting to secure a safe route. The men had neither days nor weeks; they had to trust to their luck and strike out up the icy trail.

By great good fortune, the glacier, which Shackleton later named the Beardmore Glacier, was the way to the pole, but it was also an icy, crevasse-strewn pathway rising for a hundred miles from the Ross Ice Shelf to the polar plateau. Four men and the one remaining pony, Socks, started up the glacier, detouring around obvious crevasses but unable to avoid falling into others. Falling into crevasses was at times an hourly event for one or another of the party. Thus at any moment one or every member of the party could fall to his death. The ice could swallow the entire group and no trace would ever be found. Yet they pushed on, counting on fortune's favor.

That grace ended suddenly. On 7 December 1908 tragedy struck. The three men in the lead heard a cry from Wild, who was leading Socks and a sledge. They turned around to see only Wild and the sledge. A snow bridge over a crevasse suddenly had given way under Socks, plunging him into a hole so deep the men could not estimate its extent. The men stared down and listened but caught no sight or sound. Wild had been lucky; had not the attachment between him and Socks broken, Wild would have shared the pony's fate.

Disaster loomed. The death of Socks created three problems. They would have to manhaul all equipment earlier than planned. The loss of the meat of the last pony, upon which they had counted for two weeks of food, lessened their chances of returning alive. Moreover, the loss of the fresh meat meant that scurvy might occur earlier than the men had expected.

Without the luxury of choice, the men trudged up the glacier, dragging a thousand pounds of food, fuel, and equipment. Despite hardships they continued to gather geological specimens, including coal that Frank Wild discovered. By mid-December the possibility of failure was apparent, for they were three hundred miles from the pole and had only five weeks of food. Yet hope remained. Asleep or awake, food dominated their thoughts. For two weeks, conversation focused on their planned Christmas dinner, a feast for which extra food was put aside. They still maintained a surprising degree of good cheer, and the occasion of someone falling into a crevasse was usually met with the retort, "have you found it yet?"[10]

On Christmas day, while still on the Beardmore Glacier, they enjoyed the first full rations they had had in six weeks. The meal was a grand one by the standards to which they had become accustomed, and it fulfilled their dreams because it contained enough food to satisfy their ever-present painful hunger, if only for the moment. Moreover, the celebration was followed by cigars, creme de menthe, and plum pudding with medical brandy. Full for once, the explorers slept blissfully.

Morning brought the sharp sting of reality: 250 miles still separated them from the pole, after which they would have to return to the spot where they camped on 25 December. By reducing the already short rations so that a week's food carried them ten days, they hoped still to be able to make their goal.

Their lack of knowledge about the glacier added to their burdens; the unknown road always seems longer. Climbing ever upward, their thoughts were plagued by uncertainty about just how far they would have to ascend. They passed seven thousand feet above sea level, then eight, then nine, and still the upward glacier slope greeted every footstep. Finally, on 28 December 1908, the path ceased to rise; they had come to the polar plateau.

Starving and pushed to the edge of endurance, the party now marched in the rarefied air at ten thousand feet above sea level. Shackleton in particular was bothered by the altitude but pushed his body indomitably forward. Marshall, the physician, feared for their survival. Each had doubts about the wisdom of continuing, but Shackleton urged them forward.

Now, though, Shackleton's sledge diary betrayed his

growing concern that they would not reach the pole. Their tattered clothing bore witness to the battering their bodies were taking and barely protected them from the painfully harsh conditions. When Marshall took the men's temperatures on 29 December, Wild's temperature was 94.2°F. Wild was the only one whose body was warm enough to be measured on the doctor's thermometer; the temperatures of the others were not high enough to register. Their hunger was only half of their problem. The shortage of fuel for melting water meant that they were extremely dehydrated, making them less resistant to the outside temperatures, which were in the range of -24°F at night. Even so, they plodded on southward, endlessly putting one foot ahead of the other.

On 1 January 1909 the party passed a significant mark; they were closer than anyone had ever been to either pole. This was a great achievement, but without the pole Shackleton knew the effort would be thought a failure. On 3 January Shackleton still harbored hope of making the pole in thirteen or fourteen days. But the mathematics showed that the margin for victory was beyond thin — the pole, yes; the return, doubtful.

Everything depended on the pole — all of Shackleton's dreams: fame, enough money to secure his family's future, and triumph for its own sake. To turn back short of the goal would prove his detractors right: he would have failed. In this context, the decision Shackleton made on 6 January 1909 was the bravest act in the entire Heroic Era. Rather than risk the life of one or more of his men, he resolved to turn back. He announced that the following day they would push on without sledges far enough to be certain that they were within one hundred nautical miles of the pole, and then they would turn north.

The next morning a blizzard raged, and it continued throughout the following day. The men were frostbitten as they lay in their sleeping bags. Shackleton read *The Merchant of Venice* aloud to pass the time. Finally the ninth brought a break in the weather. The four weary men walked to where Marshall (who, significantly, was the navigator rather than Shackleton) indicated that they were at 88°23' S, roughly ninety-seven miles from the elusive pole. Having a navigator other than the leader eliminated the controversy that surrounded contemporary attempts at the North Pole.[11] By having another person as the navigator, Shackleton provided an outside source for the distance achieved. They planted the queen's flag, photographed one another, and then returned to their camp. That night Shackleton wrote in his diary, "We have done our best."[12]

The return north was a race, food ahead and death behind. En route north the party was aided by several factors. The wind was at their backs, and a sail on the sledge lightened their load. They knew the route back and so felt less anxiety about the path, although they were daily concerned about losing signs of their outward trail. With the wind coming from the south, they could converse as they marched. While their route took them through spectacular scenery that never before had been seen by human eyes, their conversation turned not to the majesty of Antarctic splendor but to food. They described great heaping meals of food in the most minute detail. The men dreamed of huge piles of fatty, lard-ridden food, with lots of butter scooped on the top. These descriptions met with equally avid responses. In the back of their sledge diaries the men made menus of meals they wanted to eat when they returned to civilization. While their sense of humor ranged far and wide and apparently never flagged, they never joked about food.[13]

They drove themselves onward over the polar plateau, knowing that they had to make each depot in the allotted amount of time or stretch their already reduced provisions until they reached resupply.

They made good time returning to the Beardmore Glacier but still ran into trouble. Breakfast on 26 January 1909 exhausted the last of their food, and they marched for forty hours over horrific surfaces toward the next depot without reaching it. Three of the four men were played out. Only Marshall had a reserve of strength, and he pushed on to the depot, retrieved food, and brought it back to the others. Reinvigorated by sustenance, the party made it to the depot just in time. Had a storm overtaken them any time during the nearly two days since their last meal, they would have died and vanished without a trace.

When it appeared almost impossible for matters to get worse, they did. Added to starvation, exhaustion, and exposure, the party was now afflicted with dysentery, and Wild was worse than the others. Apparently some of the pony meat caused the problem, and the largely meat diet was particularly hard on Wild. All the men craved grains, but their allotment of biscuits was down to one a day at breakfast. One morning as breakfast was ending, Shackleton approached Wild and pushed something into his hand. Wild knew what it was and attempted to refuse but Shackleton insisted—it was Shackleton's biscuit. Later, Wild wrote of the incident:

> I do not suppose that anyone else in the world can thoroughly realize how much generosity and sympathy was shown by this; I DO and by GOD I shall never forget it.[14]

Shackleton and his men pushed ever northward. On the way, no scrap of food was ignored. The ground at old meal stops was scoured for crumbs or pieces of chocolate. At one halt the men found a pool of frozen pony blood, which they added to the hoosh (as they called their evening stews).

A second time they ran out of food. No food remained after breakfast on 13 February. This time, though, they reached the depot in a single day. Now another potential problem loomed.

The next depot was Depot A, but when they had

marched south it had not existed. Shackleton counted on Ernest Joyce (1875–1940) to lay that depot while the main party was en route to the pole. No tracks would lead to this cache; they would have to navigate to it. One day at lunch, Wild was looking around and he saw Depot A over the horizon, by light refracted by a mirage, a not-uncommon occurrence in the Antarctic. Excitedly, the group altered their course toward the depot.

Once they reached Depot A, they should have been safe with enough food to make it back to the ship, but they were not. Five days later Marshall and Adams came down with intense stomach cramps. Wild and Shackleton could not hope to pull them both to safety. The invalids were made as comfortable as possible, and the two who were still ambulatory struck out for Hut Point, where help was to be waiting. Shackleton noted that the two incapacitated men were under thirty and that he and Wild were over thirty-five. He quipped to Wild, "It's always the old dog for the long trail."

The pair, nearly exhausted and having already walked more than 1,300 miles, trod on to Hut Point. Near the end of their journey their path was blocked by open water where they had expected ice. Shackleton wisely chose the safer but longer path around, a difficult decision given their mental and physical state.

Arriving at Hut Point, 1 March 1909, the two found no one. The reason was simple. Although Shackleton had given orders that a watch was to be maintained there until that very day, his orders had been superseded by the new commander of the *Nimrod*, F. P. Evans, who assumed quite rationally that the southern party was dead. Carrying 91 days of food, Shackleton had been gone 117 days. The conclusion was obvious to Evans, and he had no desire to risk live men and his ship by waiting for men who would never come. Evans may have been logical in his thinking, but he was not really Shackleton's man; others were. They persuaded Evans to take the *Nimrod* back toward Hut Point for one last look. When they did, fortune smiled upon Shackleton again. Though beyond the line of sight, the ship's image loomed up in a mirage. Seeing it, Wild and Shackleton set fire to the old *Discovery* magnetic hut, the smoke from which attracted the attention of the crew aboard the *Nimrod*.

Once aboard, Wild effectively collapsed. Shackleton, though he had been awake for fifty-four hours, insisted on leading the rescue of his men. Three of the strongest men joined Shackleton in the march back to Adams and Marshall. When the rescue group arrived at the camp, the "fresh" men were exhausted, and Shackleton, by force of will, nursed the sick men and made all the preparations for the return to the ship.

By 4 March 1909, everyone was back on board the *Nimrod*. Despite everything they had been through, every one of Shackleton's men was safe and sound and alive.

FOUR

From *Nimrod* to *Endurance*

Why had Shackleton failed to reach the pole? Clearly the loss of Socks, the last pony, diminished and perhaps crippled his chances. With another two weeks of food he and his men might have gone on to the pole, or perhaps not. Similarly, had he landed on the Barrier and made his camp there, as Amundsen would do three years later, Shackleton would have started nearly one hundred miles closer to his goal. He had tried and failed to reach his goal. Polar exploration yields no certainties.

When Shackleton returned to civilization, he was eager to get word to the *Daily Mail*, with which he had a contract for exclusive rights to the story. Before the ship returned to Lyttelton harbor, Shackleton slipped in at Stewart Island and sent a lengthy wire to his newspaper. Within days word of his accomplishment spread around the world. Aided by the slant of the *Daily Mail,* which proclaimed Shackleton the conqueror of the South Pole since he had nearly found the route and determined that the pole was on that lofty plain, Shackleton instantly became famous.

Feted along the route home, all doors were open to him, but he still had no assurance of the wealth he sought. His publisher, William Heinemann, was an astute businessman. He knew that for a book to be successful, it would have to be published as quickly as possible to take advantage of the potentially ephemeral fame of the principal. Heinemann hired a New Zealand reporter, Edward Saunders, to collaborate with Shackleton on the voyage back to England. Each day Shackleton would dictate for a couple of hours. Saunders typed up the material, and Shackleton immediately corrected the copy. In this way the manuscript was largely done by the time that the explorer reached England. The resulting book, *The Heart of the Antarctic,* remains one of the half-dozen greatest polar accounts. While the narrative was shaped by Saunders on every page, the real Shackleton comes through. Praising his men and sharing credit for achievements were part of his understanding of leadership.

Crowds thronged to greet the returning hero. More than ten thousand people mobbed him at Charing Cross Station when he arrived there on 14 June 1909. In the crowd was his former commander, Robert Falcon Scott, still unhappy with his former third lieutenant's failure to live up to the agreement the two had reached but urged by J. Scott Keltie of the RGS to make an appearance and welcome Shackleton home.

The next months were nearly as grueling as much of the expedition. Shackleton made a major speech at Albert Hall and then launched into a speaking tour. In November 1909, Shackleton was knighted in the Birthday Honours. *The Heart of the Antarctic* came out that fall, and Sir Ernest was ready to depart for a lecture tour on the continent.

All this success had not, however, brought him fortune. Publicly he said little about his debts from the *Nimrod*, but they were considerable, and all his lecture work was devoted to paying off his obligations. Through private sources, members of the British government learned of the financial straits of the returning hero, and a government grant of £20,000 was given to him as a reward for his job well done.

Shackleton was honored everywhere and seemingly by all classes of people. Crowds appeared wherever he went. On the continent he met with Kaiser Wilhelm II, with whom he had a cordial audience. Like so many others, the Kaiser liked the Anglo-Irishman. In St. Petersburg, Shackleton's scheduled fifteen-minute interview with Tsar Nicholas II lasted two hours.

The newly famous man spent ninety days lecturing six days a week in a London theater, retelling the story of the expedition. Fortunately he had lantern slides as well as some moving picture footage to illustrate his talks, and because of the lectures Shackleton came to appreciate the value of a good photographic record of these endeavors. Through all those performances Shackleton did not seem to mind retelling his saga over and over again.

Meanwhile, others were preparing to seize from him the mantle of temporary popularity. Robert Falcon Scott had announced an expedition and by the summer 1910 had departed England on the *Terra Nova* to continue his scientific work and to reach the South Pole.[15]

Relations between Scott and Shackleton were strained. Because Shackleton broke his promise not to use McMurdo Sound as his winter quarters for the *Nimrod*, Scott felt a righteous indignation against his former lieutenant. That this feeling was complicated by some degree of envy and resentment of Shackleton's success may, in Scott's mind, have clouded the relationship. Shackleton regarded Scott as part of his past, a chapter he would as soon forget. However, he also felt a sense of guilt over the promise he had been unable to keep.

Soon, another figure was on the Antarctic stage. Roald Amundsen, who had to be counted among the premier explorers of the day by virtue of his first successful completion of the Northwest Passage, had raised funds to make a voyage to the Arctic. There he planned to freeze his ship in the water and drift across the Arctic Ocean doing scientific research. At the right moment he expected to leave the ship and travel over the ice to reach the North Pole. He was preparing to leave in 1909–10 when a problem arose. Both Robert E. Peary and Frederick A. Cook claimed to have reached the pole, the latter in 1908, the former in 1909. Now Amundsen's hook for attracting funds was gone, and he secretly changed his plans. He would still go on the Arctic drift, but while traveling around South America he would make a detour: he would make an attempt on the South Pole.

News of this change of plans was conveyed by Amundsen's brother to Scott and by the latter to the world. Shackleton now had two competitors, one of whom would likely eclipse him as the Antarctic hero of the hour.

Shackleton still did not have financial security. Like many who are driven by an overwhelming monetary need but lack the business expertise and the mindset to achieve their goals, Shackleton bounced from one project to the next hoping to find something that would make him comfortable. To be rich was never the goal; freedom from money worries was.

Knowing that either Scott or Amundsen would soon become the darling of the lecture circuit, Shackleton kept going at it himself as long as possible. His agent even sent him to the United States to make a speaking tour there.

Shackleton had openly considered giving up exploring. He knew his health was not excellent; he suffered from occasional recurrences of the shortness of breath and the heart pains that had visited him during his polar journeys. Publicly he denied every suggestion that his health was less than perfect. He would not allow a doctor to examine him and made up strange conditions such as "suppressed influenza" to explain what was wrong.[16]

Shackleton was planning another expedition to Antarctica "purely for scientific reasons" in association with Douglas Mawson, the young Australian who had been with him on the *Nimrod*. Mawson clung for as long as possible to the dream that Shackleton would lead the expedition and then wrote Shackleton asking for his assistance in launching an endeavor of his own; this Shackleton did to great success. Unable to provide for his own needs, Shackleton had a knack for helping others.[17] Mawson was soon on his way south on the *Aurora*, taking with him Frank Wild, who had stayed close to Shackleton in hopes of following him south again. With Mawson's offer the only assured expedition, Wild went with him as his second-in-command. Perhaps Wild would return in time to go with Sir Ernest.

Another potential rival had also appeared. The German scientist-explorer Wilhelm Filchner (1877–1957) was no lightweight. He had earlier gained fame for exploring in Asia. Now he proposed to cross the Antarctic continent in a single season.

Filchner was not the first to propose such a scheme.

William S. Bruce had the idea well formulated by 1908. At the turn of the century, Bruce was the leading British polar figure in terms of service and experience and would have made a fine leader of the scientific staff for the *Discovery* expedition had science been foremost in the mind of Sir Clements Markham. Cast aside by Markham, Bruce had launched his own privately funded Scottish National Antarctic Expedition (1902–4) to conduct serious scientific research in the South. The Scot's scheme was well conceived and well executed, and Bruce did fine work in the South Orkney Islands and the Weddell Sea. Bruce brought the Argentine scientific community into partnership with him and persuaded them to maintain his scientific station after the end of the *Scotia* expedition. Still in operation today, Orcadas base, as it is now known, holds the distinction of being the longest continually staffed post in Antarctica.

Bruce was a fine scientist and a competent leader of an academic staff, but he was not charismatic. He had the idea and the plan but could not find sufficient financial backing to make his dream a reality.

Although Bruce was no longer in the running, Filchner had the funding, a good ship, and perhaps the wherewithal to accomplish the task. Shackleton might well ponder, what would be left for him?

In addition to all these concerns, Shackleton faced another major problem: his brother Frank's legal difficulties. The story of Frank Shackleton lies beyond the scope of this narrative; it is sufficient to note that Frank, who had pretensions to being a financial advisor and investor, had skirted the law on several occasions. He was rumored to know a great deal more about the theft of the crown jewels in 1907 than he would admit. Finally, after engaging in a number of questionable practices, he was arrested on charges of misappropriating the funds of a client. He was found guilty and sentenced to fifteen months at hard labor. This family crisis added to Sir Ernest's concerns.

Sir Ernest's own financial circumstances were strained. Shackleton's wife's income just about covered their household expenses, but at various times in the period 1910–13 Shackleton was forced to borrow from friends. Having nothing of value to offer as collateral, he gave what he could, including stocks in ventures of questionable value.

Exploration was only one of several avenues of potential financial security. While lecturing in Hungary he met people who assured him that a "fortune could be made," a phrase that always caught Shackleton's attention, in Hungarian gold mines. Pursuing this dream took a good deal of Sir Ernest's time during this period in his life. Shackleton was at the same time pursuing the possibility of earning great wealth through a tobacco company that at various times he indicated he owned, although in fact he was merely a partner.

In March 1912 news of Amundsen's triumph

reached the outside world. The South Pole was gone, but Shackleton characteristically praised Amundsen and his achievement. Others in British geographical circles were not so generous. Shackleton greeted Amundsen when the latter came to England to speak. Shackleton had no ill feelings toward Amundsen for succeeding where he had failed. No detailed news of Scott appeared that spring.

In January 1913 Shackleton learned that Filchner's plans had met with misfortune and he was prevented from establishing a base to make the run across the continent.[18] The following month, February 1913, the press throughout the world carried the news of the death of Scott and his companions en route back to the ship after having reached the pole.

Shackleton had tried many things since the *Nimrod* and had been at best moderately successful. Success in other fields eluded him, and at various times he became despondent over his chances of ever being successful enough to provide security for his family and himself. In a letter written at one of those depressed moments, he wrote, "I suppose I am really no good for anything but exploring."[19]

The pole was gone, but one last great achievement remained: crossing Antarctica.

FIVE

The Greatest Adventure
of All Time

The world accepted the claims of Frederick A. Cook and Robert E. Peary that they had reached the North Pole, although in all probability neither had. Roald Amundsen's elegant planning and superb execution brought the south polar laurels to Norway, while the British could savor the knowledge that although Great Britain was in relative decline, its sons could still "meet death with as great a fortitude as ever in the past."[20] Amundsen in triumph was the man of the hour; Scott in defeat won fame for all the ages.

With the South Pole achieved, only one great Antarctic adventure remained: to cross the continent. This is exactly what Shackleton proposed to do.

While the condition of his heart was such that he would not allow a physician to examine him, Shackleton was at the height of his powers as a leader in 1914. A proven polar explorer capable of inspiring extraordinary devotion from his men, he was the ideal individual to attempt this last great geographical journey. That Bruce failed to get the project off the ground in 1908 did not mean Shackleton could not manage it. To compare Bruce and Shackleton in terms of their ability to attract financial support would be unfair—few had Shackleton's ability, and no one who knew Bruce would even put him in the same category. Bruce lacked Shackleton's bon vivant style; none of his co-workers could ever remember seeing Bruce laugh. These personal traits do not detract from Bruce's competence as a scientist-explorer. While Shackleton will never be compared to Bruce with respect to scientific ability—Bruce can be seen as the premier British subject at the turn of the century in terms of scientist-explorers—what this situation called for was not science but sizzle. Sizzle was a Shackleton specialty.

Bruce, however, was gracious when Shackleton took over his idea of a transcontinental journey and assisted Shackleton with his preliminary preparations. Long-term planning was never a strong suit of Shackleton, who counted on his ability to pull everything together quickly and with an appearance of nonchalance. He often succeeded with such an approach.

By 29 December 1913 Shackleton had sufficient financial backing to announce his plans and moved to assemble equipment and men. Most importantly, he needed a ship.

In Sandefjord, Norway, a group of backers including Adrien de Gerlache (1866–1934), who had led the *Belgica* expedition (1897–99), had commissioned a ship to take tourists to the polar regions. The vessel, then named *Polaris*, had been the favorite project of the shipbuilder, who lavished great care on the ship. Then the deal fell through. Framnaes shipyard was left without a buyer for the *Polaris*. The special features of the vessel now proved to be liabilities: it was extremely strong but with too small a hold for use in transporting goods, for whaling, or for sealing. The *Polaris* began as a barkentine but now threatened to become a white elephant.

Enter Shackleton. The ship's disadvantages were inconsequential for an exploring ship, and its strength was a decided benefit. Framnaes and the Boss struck a deal. Now, Shackleton had his ship, which he renamed the *Endurance* for his family motto, "By Endurance We Conquer."

The *Endurance* was one hundred and forty feet long with a beam of twenty-five feet, not a large ship by contemporary standards. The *Explorer*, the original passenger expedition cruise ship that opened Antarctica to tourists, measures two hundred and twenty feet long and forty-two feet abeam.[21] But Shackleton's vessel was a fortress—one of the strongest wooden ships ever to sail the icy south polar seas. The sides of the ship were eighteen to thirty-six inches thick and made of a variety of woods—elm, English oak, and Norwegian fir. Outside those was a sheathing of greenheart, a tropical wood so hard that working with it required special tools. Greenheart was used to withstand the glancing blows of the ice. Huge cross supports were placed at regular intervals to strengthen the outside wall against ice pressure. Shackleton could be confident of the strength of his ship against all but the most intense ice pressure.

As with the *Nimrod* expedition, Shackleton showed the capricious side of his nature when choosing men. Flooded with potential applicants attracted by his fame, Shackleton was able to select from a wide number of aspiring Antarctic heroes. Shackleton knew that in selecting men for an expedition, one did not need and did not want all one type of personality. Like an orchestra conductor hearing different tones, Shackleton worked to create an ensemble.

His interviewing style would not be offered as an example in a management text.[22] He once conducted an interview by asking three questions: How are your teeth? Do you have varicose veins? Can you sing, not opera, but can you shout along with the boys? Shackleton was known to conduct an interview in the hurried seconds after he emerged from his private office and flew through the outer office in a blur and bolted into the street to a cab. Despite this haphazard approach, Shackleton made few mistakes.

Among those interviewed were two people new to the story who need to be introduced, for they played an important part in Shackleton's life and in this expedition. Tom Crean (1877–1938) had begun his Antarctic career in a most off-handed manner. When the *Discovery* was in port in Cape Town in 1901, Scott dismissed several unsuitable candidates. A call for volunteers on Royal Navy vessels in port yielded several erstwhile polar heroes. None of the new men was better or had a more distinguished Antarctic career than Tom Crean.

Onshore he had some of the same vices and proclivities as many naval men. During a royal visit to send off a party of Antarctic heroes, one of the ladies-in-waiting spotted a white ribbon among the medals on Crean's chest and timidly asked, "Is that for purity?" The rest of the men stifled a laugh. "No, miss," Crean rejoined, "that is for Antarctic service."

On the *Discovery* he had distinguished himself as a hardworking, bright, and exceptionally fine seaman. By the time of Scott's second expedition (1910–13), Crean was a petty officer, and he was promoted to chief petty officer after he returned from that voyage. Because of the strict class consciousness of Victorian England, one could not be an officer unless one was a gentleman by birth. Other men entered the navy at the lowest rank, and the best worked their way up to petty or chief petty officer. A chief petty officer could be as proud of his achievement as an admiral of his, for each had gone as far as his class origins would allow.

On Scott's second expedition Crean's character and qualities had come into clear focus. On the ill-fated south polar attempt of 1911–12, Scott opted to abandon four-man teams at the departure of the last supporting party. Before that group turned back, on 4 January 1912, Scott asked his second-in-command, Lieutenant E. R. G. R. Evans (1881–1957), if he could take one of the lieutenant's party to the pole. Evans could hardly refuse, although starting a six-hundred-mile sledging journey with only three men put the smaller party at risk.

Lieutenant Evans, Crean, and William Lashly (1868–1940) turned north from the southern end of the Beardmore Glacier. Lashly was the man whom, in retrospect, many polar enthusiasts wish Scott had taken to the pole instead of L. E. G. Oates (1880–1912) or Edgar Evans (1876–1912). Lashly was strong, dependable, and bright. He could turn his hand to any task. Before the 1911–12 season was over, Lashly had sledged farther than anyone else in Scott's expedition. Having turned forty-four during the southern advance, Lashly was the oldest man on the ship.

The three-man party struggled northward, but it was soon apparent that Lieutenant Evans was suffering from scurvy. His health deteriorated rapidly and threatened the lives of all three men. Evans began to have difficulty getting himself dressed or pulling in the traces, for the men were manhauling. Evans continued to deteriorate; Crean and Lashly were forced to help him with everything. They dressed him in the morning; later, as he deteriorated, they cleaned him when he soiled himself. When Evans could no longer walk, the other two put him on the sledge and pulled him, but at a pace that threatened to prevent them making each return depot on schedule. Falling behind in meeting each depot on time meant one thing to all: death. Only Evans could navigate. Evans knew that he had to stay alive until his men could see physical features they recognized indicating the way back to the hut. One morning one of those features came into view, and Evans knew he had done his duty—he had gotten his men to a place from which they could find their own way home.

Evans did the right thing. That morning he called his men over and ordered them to leave him and continue on to the ship without him. Crean and Lashly were shaken. They had lived their entire lives obeying the orders of their officers. Retreating a short distance from Evans, they held a council. Returning to their officer they told him, "We're sorry, sir, but we cannot obey that order." They put him on the sledge and hauled him back nearly to the ship.

By 18 February 1912, two factors brought their situation to a crisis. Weakened by the efforts of pulling Lieutenant Evans, Lashly and Crean had increased difficulty making depots on time. Evans was failing fast and would likely die within a few days. A second council was held. One had to go for help while the other waited with the lieutenant. Crean did not want to be with Evans when he died, so Lashly stayed behind while Crean, fortified with only a few biscuits and some chocolate, struck out alone across the frozen Antarctic wastes in hopes of reaching the hut (and help) before a blizzard overtook and killed him. Lashly knew that if Crean did not return, not only would Evans die, but Lashly would too. Lashly did what he thought was his duty.

Crean made it, but just barely. Within an hour of his arrival at the hut on 19 February, whiteout conditions enveloped the station. When it cleared, a rescue party went out to relieve Lashly and was able, by a thread, to save the lieutenant's life.

For this act of uncommon heroism, Crean and Lashly were awarded the Albert Medal, the highest award in the gift of the Crown for bravery in civilian circumstances. On ice or sea, Crean clearly was a man on whom you could depend, whatever the situation. Shackleton knew this, and by the end of this story everyone else would too.

Another central character to the story was Frank Worsley (1872–1943), a New Zealander and a ship's captain by profession. One night while in London between ships, Worsley dreamed that he was piloting a ship through huge blocks of ice—but the ship was in Burlington Street in London. Unnerved by the experience, the Kiwi went the next morning to Burlington Street, and there he saw the sign, "Imperial Trans-Antarctic Expedition." Worsley went in and told Shackleton of his dream. The Boss replied, "You're going with me." Before the expedition was over, the lives of every man on the vessel would depend, not once but several times, on the extraordinary boat-handling and navigational skills of Frank Worsley.

Amazingly, the thousand-and-one details necessary in order to launch an expedition like that of the *Endurance* were brought to some resolution by August 1914, and the vessel was ready to depart. King George V (r. 1910–36) and Queen Mary visited the *Endurance* before departure. The queen gave Shackleton a Bible, and the whole royal party enjoyed their visit. The ethereal nature of a royal visit gave the right degree of luster to the departure.

Then, reality overwhelmed them. In that month, the great powers were concerned with issues other than Antarctic exploration—Europe was on the verge of war, and Great Britain was engulfed in the struggle.

Shackleton called his men on deck, informed them of the situation, and all agreed that the right thing to do was to volunteer in this time of crisis to serve King and Country. A telegram was sent to the Admiralty volunteering ship and company to the war cause. The response came as a single-word wire: proceed. The message came from the First Lord of the Admiralty, Winston S. Churchill.

Shackleton sent Worsley to Buenos Aires with the ship while the Boss remained behind to raise additional funds, for once again Shackleton was desperately short of money and creditors were hounding him. Shackleton sailed by steamer to Latin America and joined the ship in October. He opted to depart Buenos Aires for South Georgia on 26 October 1914.

Once at sea, Shackleton became a changed man. Casting off civilization, he returned to his element, his spirits brightened, and his burdens lightened. Shackleton's real personality emerged at sea after months of dealing with creditors and financial problems.

The ship was three days out of Buenos Aires when a stowaway was found and brought up to face the ire of the Boss. Some on deck might have expected Shackleton to take a lighthearted approach to the situation; after all, the ship could use another hand. Instead, Shackleton turned on the young lad with a ferocity that surprised many on deck. Shackleton tore into the poor boy and subjected him to a barrage of foul language that would have peeled the wallpaper in a Victorian living room. Even the sailors were impressed by the tone and color of Shackleton's remarks. The boy, however, was not the object of this tirade; he was merely the catalyst. To bring a stowaway aboard was a degree of insubordination, and Shackleton knew that on the kind of endeavor in which they were engaged they could only have one leader—him. Shackleton's outburst reflected not a vainglorious desire for self-aggrandizement but instead the fundamental and internalized realization that in the long run the life of every man aboard would depend on their faith in him as a leader—and on his ability to command. Shackleton was fanatical about preserving the lives of his men, a goal that he perceived to be the most important aspect of his leadership. The boy before him that day was just a means to demonstrate these ideals to the others on the deck.

The exchange took a strange turn at the end. Shackleton stopped, paused, and then went at the boy again. "On expeditions we sometimes run out of food, and if we do, you'll be the first to be eaten." The terrified youngster sheepishly responded from unknown depths, "Well, sir, you look like you'd make a better meal than me." Shackleton had to turn to hide his smile. Eventually the youngster, Percy Blackborrow (d. 1949), signed on before the mast and became a valuable member of the crew.

The *Endurance* pushed on toward South Georgia Island. Shackleton had two reasons for choosing this destination. He still needed polar equipment and supplies, and Filchner's expedition had left behind equipment that Shackleton hoped to acquire. Perhaps of equal importance was something *not* available in South Georgia—contact with the outside world. The wireless did not extend that far. Once at sea Shackleton could not be recalled. The further the Boss got from possible interference by others, the more he came to depend on his own resources, and with that came a sense of quiet confidence.

Arriving in Grytviken, South Georgia, on 5 November 1914, Shackleton soon discovered that the whalers had words of caution for him — this was a bad year for ice. The whalers, experienced men who knew how dangerous the ice could be in the Weddell Sea, advised Shackleton to delay his departure in hopes that the ice pack would clear.

C. A. Larsen (1860–1924) had first visited the Antarctic in the 1890s and had seen the commercial potential for whaling. Grytviken was the first of the whaling stations to be established in South Georgia when C. A. Larsen's company began operations on 22 December 1904. Whales were plentiful in the first season; indeed, during the first year most whales were killed *without* leaving Cumberland Bay. The whalers were limited in their killing only by the inability of the coopers to make barrels for the oil quickly enough. Whaling was a hard life, and only great profits encouraged people to continue in the industry.

Shackleton passed a month at Grytviken, no doubt walking through the surrounding area, passing the little cemetery that overlooks the bay, or visiting the church Larsen had had dismantled in Strømmen, Norway, transported to Grytviken, and reassembled there.

Finally, on 5 December 1914, the *Endurance* cast off from the harbor at Grytviken and headed south into the Weddell Sea. The whalers' warning was soon verified, for the party encountered ice at an unusually low latitude, 59°28' S. Looking to the past for a precedent brought no comfort. The only ship that had found ice at such a low latitude was C. A. Larsen's *Antarctic*, which had subsequently been beset and crushed by the ice in 1903. For his part, Worsley had never seen pack ice and was fascinated. For a month the talented skipper skillfully piloted the vessel through leads of open water, now advancing, now retreating, now seeking protection in the lee of a large iceberg.

By mid-January 1915 the chances for a successful landfall were doubtful, as was the possibility of escaping from the ice's grip. Briefly nipped by the ice, then released, the ship maneuvered forward, but finally on 18 January the ship was beset. Hope continued for another three weeks, but when the ship was beset on 27 January, Shackleton and Worsley accepted their fate and ordered the fires in the boilers to be extinguished. The *Endurance* ceased to be a ship and became an ice station drifting with the pack in the Weddell Sea.

The currents in the Weddell Sea move in a clockwise manner along the southern shore, and once Shackleton became convinced that the ship was indeed beset, he still had a chance to land his winter party and achieve his goal. The crew remaining on the ship, however, would have been left to their own fate, and Shackleton was not one to leave his men in the lurch.

Shackleton knew both from his general knowledge

of polar history and from his instinctive ability to lead that the dark winter months held potential threats for his men. On the *Belgica* expedition (1897–99) the ship had been caught unexpectedly in the ice and the men were forced to overwinter.[23] During the polar night several of the crew had temporarily lost their reason, one permanently so, and all suffered from physical or mental problems. Shackleton's own men would be subject to the same forces of nature. Shackleton knew that to a large degree the survival of his men depended on his keeping them occupied during the winter, on his ability to persuade them to believe in him as a leader, and to some extent on the force of his personality.

Shackleton was not a man who thrived in ordinary times and circumstances; the more difficult and, indeed, impossible the situation, the more he came into his element, bringing his concentration into sharp focus on the task at hand. This quality was exactly what the men of the *Endurance* needed to survive the months ahead.

The winter was not terribly severe, and Shackleton made sure the men kept busy, their minds on their work rather than on the potential problems they might face. Winter temperatures were not extreme by Antarctic standards, and the *Endurance* made comfortable quarters.

Two possibilities presented themselves. The ship might drift with the pack and then in the spring, during the summer, or even as late as the early fall be released as the pack was broken up by the winds and the currents. Such had been the fate both of the *Belgica* and the *Gauss* (1901–3). The second possibility was more frightening. The ship was safe as long as the ice was solid and surrounded the vessel with a large floe. The problem would come in the spring. Then, the ice would begin to move, and the giant floes would start to crash into one another, rafting up huge fields of ice two meters thick. If a ship, even the *Endurance*, were caught in this process, it would be crushed. Were that to happen the twenty-eight men would be alone on an ice floe with no ship, with the nearest help more than a thousand miles away, and no relief ship likely to search for them. On top of that, they would be facing potentially the worst weather in the world. This was exactly what happened.

In the spring the ice began to press on the ship. The mighty *Endurance* at first resisted the ice that pushed against its sides. As the weeks wore on, the ice was relentless, scraping, pushing, prodding, crushing. By October the ice was forcing the massive walls of the vessel inward and causing the huge crossbeams to buckle. Leaks appeared. Shackleton's carpenter, Harry McNeish, worked tirelessly to plug the leaks and control the water damage. Man and vessel struggled against the ice but the ice won. By the end of October the ship was being twisted and bent. The deadly pressure of the ice continued ceaselessly.

Events in late October demonstrated two possible

reactions to the situation the men now faced. On 24 October 1915 several of the crew were on deck looking over the railing of the ship when a group of emperor penguins approached. Innately curious, the birds peered up at the vessel and the creatures on it. Then suddenly the birds began to sing what for all the world seemed to the men to be a funeral dirge. One man turned to the others and said, "You hear that, none of us will ever get out of this alive."

The second possible reaction was Shackleton's. As the situation became more desperate, he came into his element. On 27 October he assembled his men on the ice and told them what each must have already known in his heart: they were going to lose the ship. Then Shackleton told them they were going to effect their own rescue. Shackleton put the issue directly: "We have lost the ship and now we are going home." He warned them of the need to limit the weight of their personal equipment as they would be pulling their boats across the ice. The men had to pare down what they took; Shackleton allowed each man two pounds of personal materials and urged them to take practical things such as extra socks or mittens. He exempted their journals from the weight restriction, not for any vainglorious desire to see the expedition live on in history but because he realized the psychological value of that most personal of possessions. Everything else was superfluous. With that, he opened the Bible that had been given to him by Queen Mary and tore from it the page containing the twenty-third psalm and then placed the Bible on the ice. He then reached into his pocket, took out a handful of gold coins, threw them on the ice, and walked away.

The journey ahead was daunting. Hundreds of miles from the nearest help, Shackleton and his men would have to drag their boats across the pack ice until they reached the end of it. Then they would launch them and, avoiding the floes that could crush their tiny craft like an egg shell, sail into open water and try to reach either the Antarctic Peninsula or Snow Hill Island, the site of Otto Nordenskjöld's (1869–1928) 1901–4 expedition. A hut and supplies remained in place there.[24]

The ice near the ship was not sufficiently solid to allow a long-term stay. The men and their dogs began to drag the equipment and two of the boats. Pack ice is not smooth. The movement of the ice causes floes to crash into one another, and the result is that huge blocks of ice are piled on top of one another. The party had to hack a path through the ice to create a trail for the boats. The work was exhausting. The men proceeded for two days to a piece of ice that was at least two years old upon which they would be safe from the pressure of other ice. Here the party would wait and drift with the current, hoping it would take them toward their goal but aware that it might sweep them in a circle, past all the possible havens only to break up in the spring and deposit them in the middle of the vast Southern Ocean. Thus began their wait at what the group called Ocean Camp.

Several possible scenarios now loomed for Shackleton and his men. The ice might drift in a circle and eventually melt beneath them. Alternately the floe could survive through the summer, and the party would have to overwinter on the ice. This latter option made the others look better. A third possibility existed: the floe might bring them near enough to land for the men to launch the boats and sail to the Antarctic Peninsula or one of the outlying islands. Otherwise, their only choice was to make a dash for land over the ice, manhauling what they could manage. This route would eventually mean hopping from floe to floe or ferrying all men and equipment over open leads. Of the choices, the third was the most appealing, for it was the shortest of the long shots.

Shackleton and his crew spent two months at the site with insufficient work to divert their minds from the dangers and discomforts they faced. Shackleton had already set the tone for his men's actions. Ever solicitous of their needs and extremely mindful of the benefits, psychological as well as physical, that accrue from full stomachs, the Boss kept his men well fed. Shackleton, ever the optimist, liked the same qualities in others and encouraged positive thinking in his men.

Shackleton was open in his decision making process and accessible to all, thus giving every man a sense that he was participating in decisions affecting his life. Shackleton also worked to maintain a personal relationship with his crew, talking with each of them and showing an appreciation of each man's situation.

During the stay at Ocean Camp the men retrieved other equipment and supplies from the ship. The ice would not yet allow the mangled *Endurance* to slip from its grasp; the twisted wreckage remained at the surface until 21 November 1915. By cutting holes in the side of the ship to gain access, the men were able to scavenge everything from flour to nails in the dark and icy hulk.

During this time the photographs of Frank Hurley (1885–1962) were rescued. Shackleton was not unaware that, as with the *Nimrod*, he would probably have to make a speaking tour after the expedition and he knew the value of photographs. Hurley and Shackleton sat on the ice and opened each sealed tin of photographic negatives. Hurley was allowed to take one full tin with him. Carefully choosing from the artistic collection that he had created with such care, the photographer selected the ones to keep. Then, to guard against an urge to try to return and salvage any more, he smashed to pieces each rejected glass negative on the ice.

By mid-December Shackleton's concern for the psychological well-being of his men and the deteriorating conditions of the ice prompted a move. He announced that Christmas would be celebrated early, on

22 December 1915, with a great feast. Shackleton always believed in the value of dealing with people on full stomachs. On 23 December they would march, taking direct action to effect their rescue. Now, the goal would be Paulet Island.

For five days the men pulled and pushed their sledges and boats across the jumbled ice surface. In five excruciatingly difficult days, they managed to go about nine miles. A brief rebellion developed. McNeish, the carpenter, claimed that since the ship was lost, he no longer had to obey the orders of Shackleton or his lieutenants. McNeish's independent stand might have encouraged others to be led astray. Shackleton moved immediately to crush the uprising.

After concocting with Wild and Worsley some of the missing details of his story—one which, as H. R. Mill might have put it, was true in the larger context—Shackleton read out the articles that the men had signed and noted that he, Shackleton, had signed on at Buenos Aires as master with Worsley as sailing master. Under the terms of the contract, the men had agreed to follow the leader's orders on sea or otherwise. McNeish was isolated and the rebellion quelled.

Shackleton, realizing the futility of pushing on, called a halt to the march on what appeared to be a solid ice floe. Now, he was once again forced to do something that was extremely difficult for him—he waited.

The men called their new home on the ice Patience Camp. For more than three months, from 1 January to

9 April 1916, they watched and waited as the ice floe on which they were living drifted north and became smaller. One question was paramount. Would the floe split and toss them into the sea before they had a chance to launch their boats, or would they starve before that first fate overtook them?

The mood of the party during the time at Patience Camp was remarkably upbeat; whether because of Shackleton's optimism or his men's own confidence that somehow, no matter how long the odds, the Boss would lead them out of danger, their mood remained positive.

For some time Worsley had been urging that the third boat, which had been abandoned, be brought up to Patience Camp for use if and when the time came to put all the men in boats. A third boat would lighten the load in the other two *and* spread the men over three vessels in case one came to disaster. Shackleton agreed, and the third boat was manhauled to the camp. Other items, too, were brought up, including part of the *Encyclopedia Britannica,* everlastingly fine reading under such conditions.

Shackleton observed his men carefully, attentive to changes in their health, both mental and physical. He watched over them with great care, and nothing was more likely to elicit a stern look from the Boss than one of the men doing something foolish that might result in an injury. Caution was rewarded; no one was seriously injured in this stay and no man was lost.

Shackleton kept his own emotional strain under tight rein during the day—gone were the flashes of temper. Now all was on an even keel, but at night the Boss's tent mates occasionally were awakened by his crying out in his sleep from nightmares. Once awakened, Shackleton was restless until he worked out a solution to whatever problem had precipitated the bad dream.

By February food supplies were running low. While game was present, Shackleton was surprisingly cautious about laying in great stocks of meat. Perhaps he feared that gathering in enough food for the winter would persuade some of the men that overwintering was indeed their fate, and the negative emotional result would outweigh the safety gained by the additions to the larder. Some of the men worried about food supplies more than others, but all were aware of the need for adequate food to maintain their strength. From now on, as long as they were on the floe, food supplies were limited and rations restricted except for brief moments when a seal or another animal brought a temporary increase in their supplies. At one point when food was running low, the men shot a leopard seal, which provided more than a thousand pounds of meat. In addition, inside the animal's stomach the men found fifty undigested fish, which they ate for lunch the next day.

The size of their floe and its rafted surface, unfortunately, meant that the men had little opportunity for exercise. That meant that when they finally had to spring into action, they would be less likely to be in shape to do what they had to do. Shackleton could do little to change this.

The men passed the time as well as they could. Some played cards or other games; many read. Worsley specialized in polar history, which was not an esoteric pastime in their circumstances. Shackleton played cards, went for walks (often alone), and kept up conversation with his tent mates. Unbelievably, the talk often turned to planning future expeditions. When all other topics flagged, his companions knew one topic that was certain to bring Shackleton to an emotional peak: treasure hunting. True to his never ending desire to find both financial security and adventure, Shackleton loved to talk about various buried treasures and how to find them. Shackleton's main occupation, though, was looking after his men and planning for the future. The Boss consulted regularly with his principal lieutenants, Worsley and Wild, and planned for every contingency.

Wild was ideal for his role. Everlastingly optimistic about Shackleton's abilities after the South Pole attempt in 1908–9, Wild's devotion to Shackleton knew no bounds. Wild had unlimited confidence that, regardless of what the Antarctic threw at them, Shackleton would find a way to pull them through it. Wild's prior Antarctic experience was of great value. He was already well on his way to being the most experienced explorer of the Heroic Era in time served. So long as he was far from drink, he could be depended on to accomplish any task.

Life continued to be cold, damp, and miserable for the men on the ice floe. Sleeping bags and clothing, once wet, were dreadfully hard to dry. The men did not so much *wear* their blubber-coated clothing as they *lived* in their filthy outfits day and night, week in, week out. No amount of confidence or hope could mask the reality that they were living on an ice floe that sooner or later would melt. Procuring food was a catch-as-catch-can affair, and the men had no assurance from week to week that supplies would be replenished.

The floe continued to drift northward. On 9 March 1916 the men felt for the first time since the *Endurance* had been beset something that must have stirred their hearts as sailors—the swell of the sea beneath them. Their heads told them that this meant that while they might soon be taking to the boats, the danger was now greater that their floe might prematurely disintegrate. For success, Shackleton needed to launch the boats at just the right time. If they were launched too soon, they might be crushed by the next piece of ice that bore down on them; if too late, the men might be tossed into the sea to die.

By mid-March they were within sixty miles of Paulet Island. In 1903 C. A. Larsen had lost the *Antarctic* twenty-five miles from that island and had managed to pull his boats to the edge of the ice and then sail to safety. He and his party had overwintered there in passable comfort. The hut Larsen's men had built was still there, stocked with supplies for a future group of castaways. Shackleton still hoped that his would be that party. One of the small ironies of life was that Shackleton had had a small hand in selecting the stores that might await him at Paulet Island. For now, however, the time was not right to launch the boats. Impatient as he was by nature, Shackleton was guided throughout the entire time on the floe by an almost pathological desire to bring all of his men out of this horror alive.

By 22 March Shackleton's men were opposite the northern tip of the Antarctic Peninsula, but the ice conditions were too risky to make a run for it in the boats. The danger of losing a boat to the ice pack was too great. Unable to avoid a decision any longer, on 30 March 1916 Shackleton gave the order to kill the remaining dogs. The men ate the dogs. Then they ate the dogs' food. Still the ice floe drifted northward. By this time the party was short not only of food but of blubber for fuel, for few seals had come into range of the hunters. A lack of blubber meant that the party risked dehydration as well as starvation.

April began well. Although a series of potentially ominous cracks had opened in the floe on which Shackleton's men were camped, seals reappeared, and food and fuel were again in adequate supply. The swell, however, was rapidly reducing the size of their floe. By 4 April their little piece of ice, all that kept them from a cold and quick death in the south polar ocean, was barely large enough for their camp. Shackleton knew the decision to launch the boats could not be delayed much longer.

Now that they had drifted past the peninsula and Paulet Island appeared to be out of reach, only two more islands stood between them and the utterly empty ocean beyond—Elephant and Clarence islands.

Shackleton's men were well rehearsed. The Boss had insisted on regular drills to assure a prompt and safe launch of the boats at a moment's notice. Now, 9 April 1916, that time had come.

In the early afternoon of that day, Shackleton at last gave the order: into the boats. The men scrambled into the little craft, and the small flotilla pushed off the ice and into the ocean. Their two-thousand-mile drift had come to an end.

SIX

Into the Boats

The three tiny craft were not meant for sailing in open water. The men were dressed in land clothing. To say that they were without adequate foul weather gear would be to state the obvious. Shackleton's crew had been in the same clothing for six months. At least the coating of blubber smudge, which turned their clothing black, provided some resistance to the wind and weather—although it offered little protection.

The first day the three boats moved among the floes; the men were mindful that a single mistake could mean death. Shackleton was in charge of the *James Caird*, destined to become one of the most famous small craft in the history of polar exploration. Worsley, whose brilliance in sailing small boats was to become daily more evident, commanded the *Dud-*

ley Docker, while Hubert Hudson was in charge of the *Stancomb Wills*, the smallest of the three tiny vessels. Tom Crean was aboard the *Stancomb Wills* and gradually assumed an ever larger role in the operation of that boat. That evening they pulled up to an ice floe to camp. In the daylight the dangers were obvious; to be on the water at night would be foolhardy.

Shackleton set a watch to guard the floe and warn the men if it began to break up. While the others slept, the guard kept a lookout. Each time one of the crew went by Shackleton's tent, the Boss spoke to him. Shackleton could not, or did not, sleep.

In the middle of the night the worst happened — the floe split. The guard sounded the alarm, and Shackleton was out of his tent in a flash. Looking to one side he saw the crack open beneath a tent. He could see that inside the canvas was a man. Shackleton rushed to the tent, ripped it open, and in a single gesture reached down into the water and jerked the man, still in his sleeping bag, back to the ice floe. They walked the soaked man around until his wet clothing froze on his body, providing some protection from the elements. The rest of the party huddled up as well as they could until the morning light allowed them to regain the boats and resume their struggle to reach one of the two islands.

On 10 April 1916 the flotilla emerged from the protection provided by the pack ice and into the furor of the open sea. The rough weather buffeted the boats.

Men who were accustomed to enduring long periods at sea became sea sick. That night Shackleton ordered the other two boats to follow him back into the pack for safety. The parties pulled up on a floe, and the cook prepared a hot meal, which partially restored the crew.

Throughout the long stay on the ice floe one man had escaped the boredom of a life without work or purpose. J. C. Green had been fortunate as cook to be able to devote the whole of his energies to preparing the meals throughout their confinement on the ice, and now on scattered tiny ice floes at sea, he proved himself "a master of superb cuisine under difficult circumstances."[25]

The men passed another agonizingly cold night in wet sleeping bags as they shivered rather than rested. The next morning Shackleton could not launch his boats. In the night ice had drifted up to the floe on which they had been sleeping, and this action made it impossible to get the boats away from the ice floe. Shackleton ordered the men back to their bags to try to sleep a little longer. Nature struck: their iceberg floe split, temporarily separating the party into two groups. Undaunted, Shackleton managed to get everyone back onto a single piece of ice.

In the afternoon the barrier around their iceberg opened just enough to allow the launching of the boats. The men scrambled into them, pushed off, and were gone. When darkness fell, Shackleton decided to try to spend the night in the boats. The group stopped by a floe long enough for Green to cook a hot meal, and then they were off again.

In the morning, the sun appeared for the first time since they took to their boats. Instantly Worsley was at it, taking a sighting and figuring their position. He signaled Shackleton over to tell him the result. Despite sailing and rowing for three days, the current had taken them the opposite way, and Shackleton found himself farther from Elephant Island than when he had first put the boats in the water. Shackleton took the news calmly and gave his men a vaguely worded report—they had not made as much progress as they had hoped.

One of Shackleton's great strengths in impossible situations was his ability to shift plans at a moment's notice, with no second thoughts about his new decision. When he launched the boats, he hoped for Elephant Island. Then when conditions changed, he altered his course for the northern end of the peninsula. Now with the change in weather and currents, he changed the goal again back to Elephant Island.

They spent the fourth night in the boats. Without proper food and with completely inadequate protection from the elements, the men were reaching a state of exhaustion. Moreover, many were plagued by diarrhea. To relieve themselves they had to hang over the edge of the boat; to clean themselves they had only small pieces of ice. In addition, owing to their rapid departure from the last landing place, the men were short of fresh water. Dehydration complicated all their problems. By 13 April, Shackleton looked around him and saw men he feared would die of exposure if he did not soon get them to land.

Shackleton never faltered. He made himself visible to his men in the other boats by standing in the *James Caird*, visibly as well as emotionally their leader, inspiring confidence in all. That night Shackleton ordered that the three boats be tied to one another, so great was his fear that one might be lost in the night.

The morning of 14 April brought the alarming news that Hudson had collapsed; fortunately Crean was aboard to take over piloting the craft. Worsley was confident that he was near Elephant Island, but the clouds hung low and the land was not visible. Then on the fifteenth they saw their goal: Elephant Island. They could not land, however, for it was too late in the day to risk it, and Shackleton held off for the better light of dawn. All through the night Shackleton kept hold of the line from the *Stancomb Wills* to be sure the little boat would still be with his the next morning. With the dawn, Shackleton prepared to make his landing, but when he looked around him, he could only see the *Stancomb Wills*; the *Dudley Docker* was gone.

Shackleton pushed on to an outcropping of land, Cape Valentine, and with the smaller *Stancomb Wills* to scout the route, the two craft made it to shore. The men walked onto the shore with a sense of awe and jubilation that could not have been greater had they landed on a far galaxy for the first time. The men momentarily reverted to boyhood as they picked up stones and tossed about rubble on the beach. It was the first time the men had been on land in 501 days. Immediately the crew set upon nearby seals, and within a few minutes Green had the stove going and hot milk was prepared. Soon seal steaks were cooking for all hands.

Shackleton wondered what had happened to the *Dudley Docker*. In the night Worsley, who had been constantly at the tiller throughout the ordeal, determined that he had to rest. Giving up the tiller to Greenstreet, an experienced sailor but no match for Worsley in small boat handing, Worsley slept. Later in the night the tiny craft was ferociously buffeted by strong offshore winds. Greenstreet realized that his skills were insufficient for the task of saving the boat and called for Worsley to be awakened. The Kiwi was brought to his senses with enormous difficulty—Worsley had to be kicked to arouse him from his deep slumber—and quickly summing up the situation, he took command. He gave the necessary orders to avert disaster, and when the morning came, the *Dudley Docker* was still afloat. Unable to find a landing spot, Worsley coasted the island for several hours until he found one—the very same beach on which Shackleton had landed earlier in the day.

The party united again, the men ate and rested, then repeated the cycle. Shackleton had scarcely slept during the entire boat journey from Patience Camp. Knowing his men were safe for the moment, Shackleton slept.

Although the men were reunited, they were still not safe. Marks on the rocks clearly indicated that the small spit of land on which the men had landed would be underwater at high tide, and so Shackleton sent Wild to scout a safer haven. Wild returned later in the day with the news that a marginally better beach had been found. With great difficulty Shackleton forced his men back into the boats and the flotilla transferred to the new location, which Shackleton named Point Wild.

On the twentieth of April Shackleton assembled his men and told them what many had already anticipated. He would take the *James Caird* and sail it eight hundred miles to South Georgia Island, where help could be obtained from one of the whaling stations. A relief expedition was not likely to search on Elephant Island, and if they waited for help over the winter they ran the risk of some of the men dying from starvation or health problems. A speedy rescue was essential.

The situation for Shackleton's men was unenviable. To sail a small open boat across one of the worst stretches of water on the planet in hopes of hitting an island was their best hope. The South Shetland Islands were closer, but contrary winds and currents ruled out that possibility. South Georgia was the better choice. The men knew that the journey the Boss proposed was nearly impossible; they also knew that if any man could do it, that man was Shackleton.

With winter approaching and food supplies on the island uncertain, prompt rescue meant the difference between life and death for Shackleton's men. McNeish, the carpenter, worked to raise the sides of the *James Caird* with whatever materials were available. He also fashioned a framework over the open area and covered it with fabric. To prepare the canvas the frozen sail cloth had to be thawed over a blubber fire and then sewn. From the area where the men were working on the frozen cloth, the occasional profanity could be heard.

Shackleton's choice of crew for the open boat journey reflected his approach to leadership. He took with him McNeish because he might need the carpenter's skills and because, left on Elephant Island, he might be a troublemaker. He took J. A. B. Vincent, one of the sailors, for the same reason; he could be another potential problem if left behind. Shackleton selected McCarthy because he was an experienced seaman. Tom Crean joined the team because Shackleton knew that Crean was a man to be counted on in any situation. Worsley was the sixth man. To hit a small island eight hundred miles away in a tiny craft with limited opportunities for observation would require navigational skills of the highest order. Now indeed, the lives of every man on the *Endurance* depended on Worsley's phenomenal navigational talents.

On 24 April the *James Caird* put out to sea, taking with it the best of all that was left of their meager equipment. The men left behind stood on the shore and watched as the tiny craft with its crew, upon whom their lives depended, sailed out into the ice floes and disappeared.

Wild was left in charge of the men on Elephant Island. Shackleton could not have been more fortunate in his second-in-command, a man in whom he had complete and well-deserved confidence. Despite the occasional grousing, Wild's quiet authority was accepted by all. Among his first tasks was to create some shelter. The men piled stones a few feet high as walls and put the two boats on top as a roof. The resulting structure was about five feet high and measured ten feet by eighteen feet. Covered by sail cloth, the cracks in the wall sealed by drifting snow or ice, the hut was sufficient to keep them alive for the time being. The cook set up his stove inside. As the shelter began to warm, the men discovered that their hut was built on an old penguin rookery, the smell from which added little to their comfort. Amid the filth and grime associated with such close quarters and caused by the blubber smitch (a combination of smoke and pitch), Green did the best he could. The cook shared credit with Wild and the physicians for the survival of the party.

Wild worked hard throughout the stay at Elephant Island to maintain the optimism of his companions and to keep strife to a minimum. His wake-up call to lash up and stow, because the Boss might come today, set an optimistic tone.

Throughout their stay one controversy surfaced repeatedly. Some in the party believed that they should kill all the seals and penguins available to them to assure a supply of food throughout the winter. Wild followed the approach of his leader, who believed that doing so would send a discouraging message to many of the men: a sign that no rescue would reach them before the end of the winter, or perhaps not at all. Wild kept only limited supplies of food, which did create problems when the seals departed. Still, day by day, the men survived.

Indeed their health was fairly good. One of the men, Louis Rickinson, suffered a heart attack upon arriving at Elephant Island, but through the care of the two physicians, A. H. Macklin and J. A. McIlroy, the patient steadily improved. Another patient did not fare so well. Percy Blackborrow, the stowaway from Buenos Aires, had served as steward aboard ship but during the journey to Elephant Island had had his feet badly frostbitten. The doctors determined that an operation was necessary and ushered everyone out of the hut. The fire was stoked up and the two physicians, having nothing even remotely clean to wear, let alone any way to sterilize the surgical field, stripped to their undershirts and cut off Blackborrow's toes with tin snips.

The men passed their days as well as they could. With little real work to do, entertaining each other and themselves was their major activity. Leonard Hussey had been directed by Shackleton at Patience Camp to bring his banjo despite its weight. The small supply of books that had been saved were well used. Conversation was a pastime, although few parties as small as this one can sustain such talk at an interesting level for very long. The same stories get told over and over again, trying the listener's patience. As to the major issue in their lives—whether Shackleton would make it to South Georgia—the conversation was muted. Thomas Orde-Lees, who was something of an outsider in the group and on whom some degree of the tension of close quarters was directed, was among the rare individuals who spoke about the possibility that Shackleton might not succeed. For the most part, the men believed so completely in Shackleton that their confidence held up throughout the long weeks of waiting. Others may have complied because believing was the only real option.

At the beginning of their isolation on Elephant Island, the twenty-two men speculated that the earliest the Boss could return would be some time between June and August. Mid-winter day, 22 June, passed, then the rest of June. July followed; some surmised that the relief ship might arrive in that month. No vessel appeared. When August came and then the middle of the month passed, concern as to the fate of Shackleton increased.

Every day each man in the party went to the top of the hill and looked out at the sea in hopes of finding a ship. Every day each man walked back down from the outlook with the same message: no ship in sight.

SEVEN

The Attempt at the Long Crossing

Shackleton and his five companions on the *James Caird* departed Elephant Island. They set a course for the north before turning east in order to take advantage of prevailing winds. From the outset, this voyage was to be a struggle for survival hour by hour.

Before departing, Shackleton considered the risks involved and discussed them with Worsley, the man whose expertise was essential to make the Boss's plan a reality. South Georgia was the right choice—the winds and currents favored that destination. Shackleton was the right man to lead the party. Although some might criticize Shackleton for leaving the rest of his party, he was confident that under Wild's direction the main party would be all right. The risk was in the open boat journey. Aside from his impatience, which would have made waiting on Elephant Island intolerable, Shackleton knew that his place was to lead, to take charge of the relief operation. His men were his responsibility, and he knew that he alone would do whatever was needed to bring about their rescue.

McNeish had done an admirable job of attempting to improve the seaworthiness of the boat. The cover provided the men some protection from the elements. Shackleton had insisted, against Worsley's advice, that the ship be ballasted a little on the heavy side. That made it slower to respond and more likely to take on water, but it was also less likely to roll in heavy seas.

To navigate, Worsley had to get sights of the sun and use his chronometer to work out their location from the book of tables. The accuracy of his time piece was critical if Worsley was to guide them to South Georgia. Of the several chronometers brought on the ship from England, only one remained. Worsley wore it around his neck at all times. Even so, he had a good idea that the time indicated was not absolutely accurate but was off by as much as a minute, which would mean an error of many miles in figuring their location. In making his calculations he would have to compensate.

On 26 April 1916 Worsley got a sight, which was not an easy thing to do under such conditions. He had to be braced by his companions in order to concentrate on taking the sight. With limited opportunities to take measurements—clouds obscured the sun for much of the next two weeks—Worsley did the best he could.

Life on the little boat was miserable. From the first day they were constantly wet. Spray covered everything—man and boat. The ice built up on the surface of the vessel, and periodically one of the men had to crawl out onto the slippery deck to chip off the ice to keep the ship from becoming so heavy that it would sink.

While below, out of the wind, the men tried to sit very still so that their skin did not touch their icy clothing. If the boat lunged and a man was thrown off balance a little, the frozen clothing touched his body. Sleeping was difficult. The sleeping bags were placed in the bottom of the boat on the rough ballast rock, which was jagged and made a poor pallet. The reindeer sleeping bags were disintegrating. Reindeer hair got into everything: into the food, the water, and even the men's nostrils, which were clogged with the infernal hairs.

Cooking was difficult. Crean was the master of the technique and did all the cooking. He would brace the stove between his feet and the feet of another person sitting opposite and then balance the pot on top of that, watching constantly to prevent it from tipping over.

Shackleton insisted on regular food for his men. When he thought his companions were tired or their energy was failing, he would order hot milk between the two regular meals they had every day.

By 3 May the *James Caird* was half way to its destination. For the prior ten days the wind and seas had persistently attacked the little craft. Constantly wet, the men discovered that their skin was turning white from constant exposure to water. On 3 and 4 May the weather moderated. The men had a chance, if not to try to dry some of their equipment, at least to make it less damp. But on 5 May disaster nearly overtook them. Shackleton had just taken the tiller when he thought he saw something in the distance, perhaps a cloud. Suddenly, he realized what it was and called to his men to brace themselves against a wall of water that swept over their boat and drove it under with its force. For a moment the men feared the *James Caird* would not surface again. The tiny vessel shuddered and then rose up out of the waves. The men bailed for their lives and the salvation of their boat. Their efforts were not in vain, and both were saved temporarily.

For the next week Worsley managed occasional observations (as often as the sun came out), and the men made steady progress toward their goal. Conditions were brutal—the men were constantly cold and wet and engaged in never-ending work to keep the little craft sailing in the right direction. The cold and wet sapped their strength. Each man felt the strain, and by this time Vincent, though one of the strongest men in the expedition, had collapsed. Meanwhile

McNeish, the oldest man, held on, although for how long? Through it all McCarthy remained cheerful. The other three struggled on.

Although the men of the *James Caird* scarcely needed another crisis, by 6 May 1916 another had emerged. Their second water cask was found to be fouled. Strict rationing had to be imposed: only two ounces of water per man per day. At that rate they could not be expected to survive long. Chilled and dehydrated, not only was work more difficult, but decision-making powers were in danger of being impaired by this new and perhaps fatal problem.

On 7 May Worsley took a sight to determine his position, which, if accurate, indicated that they were within one hundred miles of the coast of South Georgia. Still, no sign of land appeared, no birds or driftwood. Could it be that Worsley was off course?

Shackleton and Worsley conferred. The goal was to strike the northern point of South Georgia so that they could proceed around the top of the island then down along the eastern side, where all the whaling stations were located. On that farther, sheltered eastern side they could expect to find help, but no settlements were located on the windward west side. Worsley had to hit that northern tip but not miss it, for nothing was beyond that point. Shackleton asked whether Worsley was certain he was on target given the circumstances of his data—after all he had had only four sights in fourteen days. Worsley replied that he believed he was accurate within ten miles. Shackleton asked him to alter his course to the east slightly to make sure they hit some part of South Georgia. Worsley made the correction.

Dawn on 8 May brought no sight of land. Overcast and foreboding, the weather allowed no easy sight of the island, even if it were there. Then, just after noon, the irrepressible McCarthy was at the tiller and from below the others heard him cry out, "Land!" Worsley had done it; in an almost limitless ocean he had found South Georgia Island.

The danger was not over. Worsley's calculations were surprisingly accurate, and they were now, with Shackleton's correction, a little south of the northern tip. The condition of the sea and the approaching darkness made it imprudent to try to land on a hostile coast that day. Despite anxiety over three members of his crew who were deteriorating rapidly and over the thirst that might easily have driven him to make an impulsive and incorrect decision, Shackleton held off. They would wait for morning to land.

Nature had other plans. The next morning, a storm overtook the little craft and threatened to blow the *James Caird* onshore. Here again, Worsley showed his mettle, making the little boat perform far beyond what might be expected of a vessel intended for much less. For nine hours, aided by Shackleton and Crean, Worsley battled the storm. Even Vincent, aroused in his weakened state, helped bail out the ship. Worsley, whose life experiences were varied, later said that those were the worst nine hours of his life as he worked to keep the *James Caird* off the rocks of both the main island and another island, Annenkov, which lies just offshore. In the end the Kiwi's tenacity and skill won out—he held the ship away from the disasters until the gale subsided. With darkness upon them again, they could rest and hope for a better tomorrow.

On 10 May Shackleton once again looked upon men who might not survive the day unless a landfall could be made. Worsley's attempt to beat up the west coast to get to the other side proved impossible. The winds and currents were too much for the limited craft. Instead, eager to make an immediate landfall, Worsley opted to enter King Haakon Bay. Gaining entrance to this bay was not easy. Worsley worked for several hours, tacking back and forth trying to navigate between the rocks and shoals that guarded the entrance to the bay. Night would soon be on them. Shackleton was determined to land and told Worsley to push on to a little cove that the navigator had noticed. On they drove past the outer barrier and into the entrance of the narrow cove at which Worsley aimed. The boat slid among the tiny rocks along the shore. They had made it to South Georgia.

To Shackleton's great fortune a streamlet was found at the location, which he called Cave Cove, and seals were nearby. Food and water seemed a great luxury to the men, and they might well have been content to let down their guard. But Shackleton would have none of it. The men were too weak to pull their boat onshore, so the Boss insisted that they unload it as much as they could to help secure it close to the land. Still unable to drag the lightened boat onshore, Shackleton decided to establish a guard over it to allow the other men to rest in a small cave at the beach. True to his leadership style, Shackleton took the first watch. Then instead of awakening Worsley for his, Shackleton took that one too.

A few hours later, the others were asleep when they were awakened by cries of help from Tom Crean, who was on watch. By the time they came to their senses and managed to get to his side to help, Crean was up to his neck in the icy water, holding on to the boat, which was drifting out to sea. The men managed to get the *James Caird* back to shore, but in the process the little boat was further strained.

Shackleton's men spent the next two days resting and gorging on the local food, including a supply of baby albatross from the cliff above their cave. Shackleton contemplated the future. The rudder of the *James Caird* had been lost as the little craft had come into Cave Cove, so sailing around to the other side of the island was out of the question. He was concerned also that none of his trio of invalids—McNeish, McCarthy, and Vincent—could take much more buffeting on the sea. He and Worsley scouted the area for alternatives. No easy solution presented itself. The loss of the rudder made even a journey by sea to the head of King Haakon Bay unlikely.

Then on 13 May, as McCarthy was standing along the narrow range of shore in Cave Cove and looking out at the mouth of the cove, he saw something: of all the places on the southern ocean to wash ashore, the winds and currents were driving their rudder directly back onto their beach. Shackleton thought it a good sign.

On the fifteenth Shackleton determined that his men were sufficiently rested to make the short run from Cave Cove to the head of King Haakon Bay. They loaded their possessions into the *James Caird* and made the slow journey up the fjord. Landing at a place that Shackleton called Peggotty Camp, from a house described in *David Copperfield*, the six men established their new base.

Given the ample food supplies, they could have wintered there and chanced rescue the following summer by a passing whaler, but time was of the essence. Shackleton knew that every day of delay in rescuing the men on Elephant Island might mean the death of one or more of them. Shackleton chose action. He, Worsley, and Crean would cross South Georgia Island on foot and get help from one of the whaling stations on the other side. Even though South Georgia was a mountainous glaciated island that had never previously been crossed and despite the fact that they had neither alpine equipment nor even a map of the interior, Shackleton resolved to traverse the island. As with the trip to South Georgia, the proposal was nearly impossible, but like that voyage, crossing was their only chance.

No amount of eagerness or desperate desire to rescue his men blinded Shackleton to the realities of his situation. He and his men were still weakened from their previous exertions, and before he could attempt this crossing, he had to do the one thing that was constitutionally hardest for him: he had to wait. He knew his men needed several days of rest and recovery before attempting this next journey. For three days they ate and slept to ready themselves.

Before departing, Shackleton gave McNeish written orders about what to do if he did not return. Noting that he had left them with adequate equipment to provision themselves throughout the winter, Shackleton instructed him that they were to await the arrival of a whaler in the spring to rescue them, as whalers would most certainly be working in the waters offshore during the coming season.

At three in the morning on 19 May 1916 Shackleton, Crean, and Worsley pushed off in the dark to cross to Stromness, a whaling station on the other side. They had the carpenter's adze, a little bit of rope, and one superfluous item—Worsley's diary wrapped in oil cloth. Shackleton opted to make a dash of it, taking neither shelter nor sleeping bag and only food enough for three days. The plan was typical of his bravado and his confidence that fortune would shine upon him when he needed it most. Starting out on this venture

Shackleton would need all the talents he brought to exploration—courage, determination, will, and luck.

The trio had to climb mountains up to 4,500 feet high. Without a map, they came to dead ends several times and had to retrace their steps. They managed to get across the narrowest part of the island but discovered when they had done so that they were well north of their intended destination. With brief rest periods they pushed on until the dawn and then the whole of the next day.

At various times progress was frustratingly slow. For a while going down one icy slope, they had to cut steps for better traction. Although Crean and Worsley asked to relieve him of this exhausting and risky duty, Shackleton insisted on cutting the steps that allowed them to proceed safely down the slope. Shackleton led by example.

With nightfall the temperature dropped. At one point it appeared they might be caught on a mountain top where they might freeze to death. Descending to a lower elevation was imperative. With deteriorating visibility making retreat more difficult, Shackleton acted boldly. Coming to a long slope, Shackleton sat down on their coil of rope and told the other two to cuddle up behind him. Then off they pushed like a human toboggan over into the abyss. With Shackleton's luck they came crashing to a halt not on a deadly rock outcrop but in some soft snow at the bottom.

They drove themselves on. The party was well beyond fatigue; they were reaching the limits of human endurance. At one point they were so exhausted that Shackleton called a halt and told the other two to sleep for thirty minutes while he stood guard. Crean and Worsley were asleep in an instant, and Shackleton fought to stay awake. Finally, fearing he could no longer stay awake, after five minutes Shackleton kicked his companions awake, told them they had slept thirty minutes, and pushed on.

All through the night of 19–20 May Worsley charted the route, although the path was often obscured by fog. By morning, when they stopped for breakfast, they were farther south along the east coast. At six-thirty in the morning they thought they heard something. Thirty minutes later by Worsley's chronometer, they stopped and listened. They heard it and this time no doubt: the whistle at the whaling station calling the men to work. It was the first sound of civilization that the trio had heard in more than seventeen months. The men did not speak at this solemn moment; they merely shook hands.

Their path took them steadily closer to the whaling station. They came to a stream that, while icy, provided the most direct path. Following the stream for a while, Shackleton and his men came to a waterfall. Slowly the three men went down the rope one at a time, over the edge and through the frigid water to the bottom. The two held the line for Shackleton, then Crean was supported by Worsley, who, having wedged the rope, quickly scurried down the rope sailor style, putting as little weight as possible on it. The rope held.

Now they covered the last stage. Coming over the rise above Stromness, they saw the whaling station spread out before them in the valley. Descending to the station, they entered it as three men from another world. Whaling stations were hardly known for their fastidious conditions: blood, blubber, intestines, and slime were everywhere. Even in this environment, however, Shackleton's party looked and smelled bad. In the same blubber- and soot-stained clothing they had worn for more than seven months, their hair long and matted with filth, the outer garments revealing the beating their bodies had taken, the trio walked up to the station manager's door.

Shackleton knocked on the door, and the station manager, without looking up from his desk, called for the intruder to enter. Then turning in his chair he saw in front of him an indescribably filthy man.

"Who the devil are you?" he asked. The figure responded, "My name is Shackleton."

Momentarily stunned, the manager soon realized the situation, and the men at the station sprang into action to help. Opening his house to his visitors, the host began to care for his guests. Shackleton and his companions soon had bathed and were outfitted from the station store. A whaler was sent around to the other side of the island under the direction of Worsley to rescue the other three men. When they arrived, McNeish was pleased to be rescued but groused that it seemed wrong that none of his companions had come over to get him in person. Worsley spoke to him; only then did the carpenter recognize his companion of so many months, whose appearance was now so radically changed by cleanliness and new clothing.

Meanwhile Shackleton had only one thing on his mind: getting a ship to Elephant Island. A British vessel was tied up at Stromness for the winter, obviously meant for the Boss's use. Shackleton commandeered it and asked for volunteers. The tough old whalers were perhaps the only people who knew the horrid conditions of the Antarctic well enough to appreciate what the trio had been through, and they were dazzled with their survival. To a man, every Norwegian volunteered to serve.

The *Southern Sky* sailed 23 May 1916 from Stromness. Five days later the vessel was stopped by impenetrable ice. Forestalled, Shackleton returned to the Falklands, where he was able to cable news of the expedition.

Back in England a rescue effort was begun even though, while Shackleton had been in Antarctica, the world had gone mad. The carnage of the First World War's western front had begun to replace the gentle world that had been lost in the late summer 1914. In England, an attempt was made to have the *Discovery*, Robert Falcon Scott's old ship, put into service for the endeavor.

Shackleton fretted at the delay. He sent urgent messages to the governments of South America asking for the loan of a ship. Uruguay responded and sent the *Instituto de Pesca, No. 1* to Port Stanley to pick up Shackleton, Crean, and Worsley for a second rescue attempt.

Departing Stanley on 10 June 1916 on the *Instituto de Pesca, No. 1,* Shackleton took this ill-equipped vessel in the direction of Elephant Island. Pushing through dangerous ice — the steel ship, if beset, would almost certainly and quickly sink — Shackleton was determined to get to his goal, but the Antarctic winter prevented him. Stopped twenty miles from his destination, with impassible ice between him and his goal, Shackleton was forced to turn back.

Returning to Port Stanley 29 June, Shackleton transferred his operation to Punta Arenas. There the expatriate British community rallied to their countryman, and a small schooner was soon chartered. A pathetically small ship, the *Emma*, was the best Shackleton could do. The result was worse than the previous attempt — a hundred miles short of his men, Shackleton was forced to turn back.

Three failures did not lessen Shackleton's resolve. Although the effort operating from England was ongoing, Shackleton wanted to rescue his men himself. To delay relieving his men while waiting for the *Discovery* to arrive might prove fatal. The Boss turned to the government of Chile. The best the Chilean government could do was to offer a steel oceangoing tug, the

Yelcho, a vessel long past its prime and no match for any serious encounter with the ice. Before the Chileans offered the ship, they asked Shackleton to promise not to take it into any ice. With irony at no premium, the Boss agreed.

On 25 August Shackleton, Worsley, and Crean departed on the *Yelcho* down the Beagle Channel into open water. This time, fortune favored the effort, and four days of clear weather and calm seas allowed Shackleton to get within sixty miles of his goal.

Near midnight on 29 August, fog enveloped the ship. Pushing on was extremely dangerous, but Shackleton asked Worsley whether he thought he could find the island in this weather. The navigator said yes, and Shackleton ordered the craft to proceed cautiously through the fog-bound waters off the coast of Elephant Island.

On 30 August 1916, one of the castaways on Elephant Island went up to the lookout, as he had every day during the stay, but this time when he looked out to sea—he saw a ship. He bolted down the little hill yelling and screaming his good news to his companions. In an instant all the men were out of the hut—knocking over the hoosh pot in the process—and were peering into the distance to try to ascertain what they could about the vessel. As the men stood there at the water's edge, one thought was on all of their minds: "I hope the Boss is all right." Then, in the little boat coming in from the ship, a figure stood up: it was Shackleton. The men onshore went wild. They were beside themselves with excitement and relief.

The boat landed, the men and equipment were quickly loaded aboard, and within an hour all were on board the *Yelcho*. In a week they were in South America, back in civilization.

Despite everything they had been through, Shackleton brought every one of his men back, safe and sound and alive.

Afterword
The Road Back Home

When the men of the *Endurance* returned from Antarctica, the reality of the Great War was not long in overtaking them. Most immediately joined their units. What can bring home the tragedy of the war more clearly than to realize that three of Shackleton's men were dead within a year? The carnage spared neither class, country, nor family.

While most of his men returned to England, Shackleton turned his attention to the rescue of the Ross Sea party, the support group that was to lay the depots from Ross Island nearly to the pole upon which his crossing party would depend to survive.

The Ross Sea shore team did a brilliant job in achieving their goal despite being deprived of their ship and most of their supplies when their vessel was blown out to sea, leaving them marooned. After difficulties with the authorities in Australia, Shackleton was able to relieve this second group of men.

Once back in England, the government asked Shackleton to travel to South America, where, using his popularity, he could solidify support for the allied cause. Later, Shackleton was called upon to give cold weather survival advice to the British government and to participate in British military actions in northern Russia.

After the war, Shackleton once again found himself at loose ends. Lecturing helped bring in some money. *South*, his account of the *Endurance* expedition, finally was published in 1919 and remains one of the great polar books.

For a while an Arctic expedition loomed as a possibility, but the deal fell through owing to lack of financial support. Instead, Shackleton opted to go south again on a scientific expedition aboard a little vessel, the *Quest*. It was a voyage made possible by the generosity of another of those benefactors who reached out to help explorers in need: John Q. Rowett (1876–1924), an old classmate of Shackleton.[26]

Joining the ship in South America in the fall of 1921, Shackleton found problems, which he immediately corrected. He could still charm, although physically his health was poor. He was glad, nevertheless, to be back on his own ship.

As they sailed from South America, the men on the *Quest* noticed an almost immediate change in the Boss.

Casting off civilization once again, he seemed more himself, but in this instance, unlike on the voyage of the *Endurance,* he was not at the height of his powers; he was nearing the end of them. In the opinion of A. H. Macklin, one of the ship's physicians, Shackleton had had a heart attack while in Rio de Janiero. Both of the ship's physicians warned him of overwork and criticized the extra work he took on himself. The old habit of caring for his men to the limits of his ability died hard, but Shackleton's body was no longer able to do his will. He was forty-seven.

On 4 January 1922 the outline of South Georgia came into view. Shackleton became excited and reminisced with his old pals. In the early hours of 5 January, Macklin thought he heard Sir Ernest in his cabin and went in to check. He found the Boss lying under only a thin blanket. Finding another cover to add to Shackleton's bedding, Macklin rebuked his leader for not taking better care of himself and urged him not to overwork himself. Shackleton responded, "You're always wanting me to give up things. What is it I ought to give up?"

Then the doctor watched in horror as Shackleton suffered a massive heart attack. Death was instantaneous. Shaken badly, Macklin went to the other physician, J. A. McIlroy, to have him come and confirm the unthinkable: the Boss's death. Nothing could have been done.

The two men went up to Wild's cabin, where the

second-in-command was sleeping soundly. Turning on the light and shaking him awake, the doctors said, "We want you to wake up thoroughly, for we have some bad news to give you—the worst possible." Then they told him: the Boss was dead.[27]

Wild assumed command of the expedition and took charge of the funeral arrangements. He decided to send Shackleton's body to South America, to be accompanied by one of his old comrades, Hussey, to England. Wild also decided that the best tribute to their former leader would be to continue the expedition as Shackleton had planned.

Hussey accompanied the body to Montevideo while the *Quest* sailed southward. A telegram brought a response from Shackleton's widow, who felt that the most appropriate place for her husband was at the site of one of his greatest triumphs—South Georgia. The body was returned to Grytviken and buried there in a small cemetery, where he lies with brave but anonymous sailors and whalers. His headstone inscription reads:

To the dear memory of
Ernest Henry
Shackleton
Explorer
Born 15 February 1874
Entered life eternal
5 January 1922

Wild brought the *Quest* back at the end of its voyage, and the men made a small memorial of their own on a point overlooking the entrance to Grytviken harbor. Standing around the little cairn, these men who had served with him knew better than any other living souls the truth of the assessment offered by Raymond Priestley, who had been on the *Nimrod* and who had observed firsthand the three greatest Antarctic explorers of the early twentieth century:

> For scientific leadership, give me Scott; for swift and efficient travel, give me Amundsen; but when you are in a hopeless situation and there appears to be no way out, get down on your knees and pray for Shackleton.

1. R. F. Scott to H. R. Mill, 17 December 1901, Scott Polar Research Institute archives, SPRI MS 100/100/2.

2. I would very much like to write a biography of Mill, but I would have little hope of publishing a volume on a figure so few people know.

3. Invernairn to Mill, 11 July 1922, SPRI MS 100/6.

4. Poor Borchgrevink suffered for years from a lack of recognition for his efforts on the *Southern Cross* expedition, although near the end of his life the RGS and others recognized the quality of his work. For further details, see T. H. Baughman, *Before the Heroes Came: Antarctica in the 1890s* (Lincoln: University of Nebraska Press, 1994).

5. Reginald Skelton, Diary of the *Discovery* Expedition, 3 February 1902, SPRI MS 342/1/2.

6. Now called King Edward Peninsula. Michael Rosove, *Let Heroes Speak* (Annapolis: Naval Institute Press, 2000), 86.

7. Subsequent research indicated that the polar party got near but not quite exactly to the pole. See Philip Ayres, *Mawson: A Life* (Melbourne: Melbourne University Press, 1999), chapter 2. Ayres has written an excellent biography of this extremely important Antarctic figure.

8. Ernest Shackleton, *Heart of the Antarctic* (London: William Heinemann, 1914), 147.

9. Shackleton, *Heart of the Antarctic*, 156, 167, 173, 177.

10. Shackleton, *Heart of the Antarctic*, 188, 193, 195, 198.

11. Who first reached the North Pole has been a matter of conjecture since 1909. For the best explanation of what happened

(and who, if anyone, got there), see Sir Wally Herbert's masterful account *Noose of Laurels* (London: Hodder and Stoughton, 1989).

12. The actual point achieved was the subject of some controversy at the time, as some members of the British geographical establishment, with singular lack of decency, challenged Shackleton's figures. Among these was Sir Clements R. Markham, the former president of the Royal Geographical Society. For Shackleton's account, see *Heart of the Antarctic*, 210.

13. Shackleton, *Heart of the Antarctic*, 232, 234.

14. Frank Wild, Diary of the Southern Journey, SPRI MS 944/1.

15. Sadly, in the rush to embrace Shackleton, many people today have ignored the heroic efforts of Robert Falcon Scott, who has suffered from two historiographical trends in this century: first hagiography and then character assassination. For a balanced view of Scott's first Antarctic expedition, see T. H. Baughman, *Pilgrims on the Ice: Robert Falcon Scott's First Antarctic Expedition* (Lincoln: University of Nebraska Press, 1999).

16. Roland Huntford, *Shackleton* (London: Hodder and Stoughton, 1985), 388, 469.

17. Huntford, *Shackleton*, 339.

18. Rosove, *Let Heroes Speak*. Chapter 21 gives a fine overview of Filchner's work.

19. H. R. Mill, *The Life of Sir Ernest Shackleton* (London: William Heinemann, 1923), 191.

20. Robert Falcon Scott, *Scott's Last Expedition* (New York: Dodd, Mead and Company, 1923), 477.

21. Tragically, the *Explorer* is no more. She sank in December 2007, an event that brought tears to many who had sailed on her.

22. Shackleton mania swept through the United States in the late 1990s and, not surprisingly, spawned a series of quick-buck volumes on management Shackleton's style. I was at dinner recently when a serious polar historian was given one of these management volumes as a gift. He opened the book to check how the author had treated one facet of Shackleton's life. He read for a minute and slammed the book closed with a disgusted look and

said, "Three factual errors on one page, how can people write this junk?"

23. Whether the *Belgica* was caught in the ice accidentally or whether it had been Gerlache's plan all along is a matter of conjecture, one for which I have seen no definitive answer.

24. The hut still remains, although it is currently used by Argentine scientists and support staff who, in January 1996, were cooking in the hut. Fire is a constant danger in the Antarctic because fire equipment, including water, is often in short supply, so the future of the hut is in jeopardy under such conditions.

25. The phrase is that of Ian Whillans, the great glaciologist whose premature death was a tragedy for science and all of us who knew and admired him.

26. The story of Rowett's involvement is well told in Michael Rosove, *Rejoice My Heart* (Santa Monica: Adélie Books, 2007). Anyone who has a genuine interest in Shackleton simply must read this wonderful account of how H. R. Mill and Lady Shackleton worked together to produce the first biography of her husband.

27. Frank Wild, *Shackleton's Last Voyage* (New York: Frederick A. Stokes Company, 1923), 64.